Secrets

of

Silence

Nikki:
Now is your Awakening!

By
Tim Williams

Contents:

Chapter 1

Insights &
Revelations
Confirmed

The Guru

The guru cannot hear your prayers even if sometimes results seem to suggest otherwise.

There was once a story about a guru who had many disciples who lived in the same town. One day he gathered them together and said he was going on a retreat for two weeks and he would see them all when he came back. After a couple of days news came to the town that an army was coming and all the men where to take up arms and fight. That night all of the devotees had the same dream which was the guru telling them that on no account should they join the army and fight because the enemy was much bigger and there would be a massacre. Astounded the devotees heeded the advice of the dream and did not go and fight. As it turned out there was indeed massacre, they had been saved by the dream. After two weeks the Guru returned from his retreat, all the devotees rushed to meet him shouting and cheering, filled with love. The guru asked why they were so excited and they told him of the dream of him telling them not to fight which had saved them. He told them 'I know nothing about this I was meditating in my cave, I knew nothing about the army or you guys having to fight.'

If you focus on the pointer and not what is pointed to then you miss the point. Unless of course you see that the pointer is what he is pointing to!

The student sometimes becomes overawed with the guru and forgets what is being pointed at and becomes obsessed with the guru end owing him with all kinds of powers that he simply does not have or claim to have. These people think that just knowing the guru will bring the utmost and no earnest effort is required. However single pointed attention on the guru and what is being said can bring immediate liberation.

If you think your guru and his way are the only way for everyone then you are deluded. He might be the only way for you, for now, though.

Very often students, devotees and those that aspire for truth have the idea that their way is the only way and that their master is the only true master and that those who do not follow their path are deluded and will not gain the true liberation. This is a manifestation of spiritual conceit and ignorance. Each person has their 'only way' and having found your only way it's something you can celebrate with others who have also found the only way even if it's not the way that you are on.

The Masters never validate your current version of yourself, they know all versions are fake. Students can waste decades trying to win that validation.

When one follows a guru who has many disciples it may happen that an old pattern of the psychological self that seeks validation as spiritual,special or accomplished may activate and one may really be making all efforts just to gain that approval and validation.The guru never gives it and the efforts expended in trying to get it generally come to nothing.If one is the disciple of a guru with few students then one is more likely to have this subtle illusion exposed.

The guru should be measured by the realisation of his students and not by the number of them.

There are some gurus who have huge events with hundreds of thousands of people attending, none of whom gain any degree of realisation and then there are less known gurus who have a small number of followers that really shine.

A true master will make you one!

Some masters do not entertain the possibility of their students ever becoming realised and so they don't. Others see that as the whole point.

The realisation of the guru can only become your understanding. Your realisation can only come from your own direct experience of what is.

Realisation cannot be given by one person to another, it is something that spontaneously arises when the causes and conditions are appropriate. The best I can get from the gurus realisation is a clear understanding but understanding is very different from realisation and it will not bring liberation.

How you get the guru is given by who you are being that he is. This is the only explanation as to why everyone gets him differently.

This is a profound truth and is true of everything not just the guru. There is no way that anything actually is yet things appear to have a way that they are. This does not emanate from the things themselves but from the one perceiving them. Everybody gets everything differently including the guru. How one gets the guru changes as who one is being that he is changes.

Some gurus intend Liberation for their students whilst other's turn their students into cash cows. These ones say "it's not what you know, but who you know!"

There are gurus who think that their status as spiritual beings is so elevated that simply by knowing them one will receive ultimate blessings and liberation after death.So while in human bodies ones role is to financially support the guru's every need. If who you are being that the guru is that he is that elevated he will appear to you that way whether or not he is that elevated to himself.

Between the guru and the devotee there can be great love even the greatest love but it is impersonal, heart in heart, directly. Even if no words are ever spoken.

The love one feels for the guru is not necessarily felt by or known to him. The fact you love him does not mean he loves or even knows of your existence. The love is impersonal and the guru is a focus point for it. There may be cases where there is close interaction with the guru that some personal love develops but chasing it is a diversion from the Path.

Without a Master or without serving with others how will your hidden ego be exposed? If unexposed it will still drive you without you knowing.

The guru has a way of exposing what is hidden, serving the guru is the ideal ground for the exposure of subtle ego and inappropriate intent. We never want to see and accept our shadow that is why we spend so much energy hiding from it and covering it up. A spiritual practitioner without a guru, guide or master has a very difficult job, some say it's impossible.

Loving the guru with full devotion is wonderful but to find the Self one must rigorously inquire within "who am I?" It's your effort and grace that take you there.

There are many who have thought 'the guru gives me liberation and it's all by his grace', making no effort they gained little. Nothing can replace what is gained by earnest and consistent effort, this puts you in the ideal place for the grace that makes all things possible.

With a mirror it's not the frame that's important but the quality of reflection. Likewise with the guru, don't think too much about their personality it doesn't matter.

It really does not matter who the guru is to himself or to others. In order for this magical dynamic of guru and disciple to work it only matters who you are being that he is, which is the only thing that will give you how you get him.

The Observer

The witness being unassociated and untouched is not impressed by great thinking, shocked by tragedy or uplifted by inspiration.

The witness is unassociated which means that nothing that is witnessed has any impact on the witness. The witness does not learn or get changed by what it sees. If one sees something terrible it is seen, as is the emotional reaction to it but the seer remains unmoved and impartial.

There is the internal commentary which names and explains from unconscious agendas and then there is the witness. Being the witness bring silence.

Until one realises and becomes the Self, the sense of a self is generated by constant internal dialogue, what that dialogue presents is given by who you are being that you are in any moment. In the unconscious mind there are various complexes that have agendas and when we are not the Self these urges drive the life and thinking. When one rests as the witness there is internal silence and clarity and the internal dialogue falls silent and the unconscious agendas are neutralised.

The witness does not evolve, creates no karma and does not ever act, it is unchanging as the sky.

In the same way that no matter what weather turns up in the sky, the sky remains untouched and unchanged by it, so it is with us no matter what internal weather conditions we experience the witness of them remains the same. There is no karma for the sky because it never does anything.The witness also has no karma because it does nothing and takes no action, it simply is. It watches the notion of karma develop in the mind, watches it play out but never generates any itself.

The observer and that which is observed only appear to be distinct.Actually the observer, the observing and that which is observed are one in the field of dreams.

When you have a sleep dream it appears that all the elements in the dream are distinct, the consciousness of the characters, the objects in the dream and the feelings you have about them. Upon awakening you realise that it was all just a dream. The characters actually had no consciousness, the objects had no substantial reality everything was made of the substance of dreams. In the clear light we see that it is the same in this waking domain.

The observer is not a real thing, it's an appearance, a temporary function of consciousness, the apparition of a false self no more real than the ego self.

The last illusion is the sense "I am" about which Buddha said "just because you have the sense that you are does not mean that you actually are!" Leaving the ego identity with all it's pain we arrive at the witness and then even that dissolves into a non localised, non centred,self cognising awareness.First find and rest as the witness, the sense 'I am'.

Can the observer be observed? As all statements are equally true, yes it can,no it can't and it neither can nor can't be observed and can both be observed and not observed!

No one perspective is truer than another, the perspective of science for example is no more real than the perspective of the hallucinator, both are figments of a dream and neither embrace the truth of what is.

It must be possible to observe the observing otherwise how would youknow you were observing.

Another view that is equally true and shows how logic can bring us to conclusions and provide the context which makes the statement so.

No you can't observe the observer, can a knife cut itself or an eye see itself or a fire burn itself.

Indisputable logic unless the observer has no similarity to a knife, the eye or fire.

In deep stillness the point of view of the observer dissolves and duality ends only self cognising Awareness remains.

Meditation shows us how the appearance of the witness is conditional and when those conditions change into deep silence the witness dissolves into omnipresent omniscience. At this point the illusion of a subject observing an object is no more.

Distinguish the observer from all it beholds, leave everything completely alone. Nothing signifies Awareness.

Leave everything completely alone means not to create anything or alter anything or do anything. Let everything be exactly as it is, this brings an enlightening experience quickly. Awareness is not signified or represented by anything, there is no sign or symptom of awareness. There are no characteristics that it has. It cannot be objectified, reified or looked at.

Where does the observer observe from? The observer is not located anywhere. Where does it watch your consciousness states from?

Awareness is equally everywhere, always,

already and it focalises as consciousness creating illusory points of view. Most observing is done visually, audibly or mentally which gives one the sense of the observer being localised in the head.Awareness is omnipresent.

When the breath is witnessed and there is no interference it will become more and more shallow until it's divine motivating principle is revealed.

The breath is then seen to arise from the heart within which is a divine principle of life, a light, the atman or soul. It is also seen that from here the sense 'I am' arises along with its thoughts.

Life beheld from the observer view point shows that everything is unfolding perfectly under Grace.

When we view life without commentary it appears as a perfect, coherent functioning.Grace in this context refers to what is inconceivably orchestrating this display.

When thoughts emotions, moods and states of consciousness arise the witness remains unaroused.

No matter what is beheld by the witness it remains unassociated and unmoved by the occurrence.The observer does not direct the attention. The observer is indifferent and impartial as to what it observes. It observes the attention and what it attends to.It sees but does not look.

The one that sees confusion is not confused by it. The one that observes understanding happen is none the wiser.

The witness is an expression or a lense of awareness it has nothing to learn or gain from the witnessing Thoughts are heard by something prior to them.The witness of your thinking is not impressed by any of it.

The observer sees but does not look, it hears but does not listen, it feels but does not enjoy. It sees the looking, it watches the listening and witnesses the enjoyment.There is no intent for the witness, no desire, no longing and no preference.

When life is seen by the witness it beholds a luminous transparency of flickering forms that have no meaning or subtantial content what so ever.

Awareness

Stages on the path, degrees of realisation, levels of attainment happen within unchanging awareness which is complete in every moment.

The Truth is ever present and unchanging Awareness, everything else happens within it and is essentially without any substantiality.

The light of awareness pervades both heavens and hells equally. This is the true Light.

The ignorant think that there is light and dark, angels and demons, heaven and hell.There is a light that has an opposite- darkness but the Light of awareness pervades all domains equally and reveals all phenomena as empty of anything substantial.This light is the ground of being everywhere.

When consciousness is united with Awareness, bliss, timelessness and profound peace prevail. Satchitand.

Consciousness is a dynamic expression of awareness and we project it out into all kinds of things and experiences but the fulfilment still alludes us until we place our consciousness onto awareness at which time we feel profound peace and stillness, joy and unconditional love as who we are.Where the mind is quiet the sense of time passing disappears and the eternal unchanging presence prevails.

Sound happens in undisturbable silence, movement happens in unmoving stillness.Form exists in emptiness, chaos arises in cosmic order.

The substratum of all phenomenal existence is awareness which is silent and unmoving as the sky. Everything is because of it nothing is without it.

The gift of consciousness is the power to attend. When attention is payed to Awareness awakening immediately occurs. Then the seeker and the sought become one.

Attention is given but where we put it that is up to us. Blessed indeed is the one who is shown or discovers how to place their attention onto Awareness, to unite their consciousness with awareness.This is the end of dualities of subject/object,perceiver and perception.

Freedom is not integrating the psychological self Freedom is not a meditation state. Freedom is recognising the self as Awareness.

There is the minds version of freedom and freedom.When everything removable is removed what remains, the essential ground of being that is boundless freedom, present within every moment.

Are you confusing consciousness and Awareness?

There is an 'I' that experiences consciousness but no "I" in Awareness.Consciousness changes, Awareness does not.There are states of consciousness but not states of Awareness. Consciousness is like weather, awareness is the sky.

All the fluctuations in consciousness, thought, mood and life drama happen in unchanging Awareness.You are that. The one who knows this lives peacefully present.

This is the ultimate knowledge, the knowing of which, through direct cognition, alone transforms our relationship to thinking and life in general.

Most people spend their lives travelling from birth to death in a continuous dream, identifying as what they do,what they have and what they think. Others seek the self and awaken in pure presence to the timeless moment.

Few are those who awaken to the luminous transparency of the Self. Realising themselves as distinct from the part they play, the roles they perform and the thoughts that they think.

Every situation and every moment offers an access to what is. You are never any distance from it. Acknowledge this and immediately it starts to unfold it's peaceful presence.

Some people think that high is nearer to real than low, but this is not the case.Others think that clarity is a mental state and never achieve it.Knowledge reality is equally near from any where just as in a dream when one wakes one sees it was all equally a dream.

Awareness holds space, awareness came first, space is multiple, the space in a dream the space in a mirror, Awareness is singular.Spacelessness.

Many mistakenly think that time and space are the bedrock of invariable reality. Time varies depending where you are, there is place where a thought takes 10 earth years to pass.Infinity between a tick and a tock. When we distinguish awareness we can see it holds space but has no size or shape.The formless takes no space.

Each sense has it's own consciousness,

When the consciousness of seeing is lifted to awareness then the luminescence prevails. When the consciousness of hearing is lifted to awareness the unstuck sound of pure presence prevails. When the consciousness of the mental sense is so lifted then there are insights, revelations and realisation.

One who knows the Awareness self enjoys literally every moment, always present he sees less and less difference, living quietly free from commentary.

It becomes clear that previously our reality and our self was built by thought and commentary but as awareness dawns we depart the world of name and form.

The intellect is eventually surpassed as the lover of truth enters the field of pure undifferentiated wisdom.

Wisdom in the ultimate sense is not conceptual but experiential, one arrives in and dissolves into pure knowingness and perfect clarity.

Discounting all states of consciousness, movements of energy, inner experiences, "not this not this "one comes to the true meditation where consciousness is merged into Awareness itself.

We come to see that awareness is ungraspable cannot be isolated and is not a thing so anything that appears is not it. By discounting more and more subtle sensations and intuitions we arrive in the stateless state.

Awareness is not peace or light or bliss. This is how consciousness manifests when approaching awareness.

Nothing signifies awareness it is quite beyond our grasp,but when our consciousness reunites with it there is light, bliss and we recognise the awareness Self through the sense of consciousness as utter stillness and peace.

Awareness is not of anything.

One is conscious of things, awareness is the all pervading substratum of unassociated isness, and there is no"I" in awareness that is aware of anything that's the temporary function of consciousness.

There is no "I am "in awareness or "my awareness."

This is a clear distinction between dynamic consciousness and awareness which is one mass, a shoreless ocean of inconceivable power, intelligence and love. Awareness generates consciousness for which an "I" is necessary. We can say 'my' consciousness but we cannot say 'my' Awareness.

Perception, cognition and reaction are functions of consciousness happening in awareness.

The temporary individual entity appears to have these functions which are aspects of consciousness manifesting in the luminous transparency called life.

The sense "I am" is a phenomenal appearance in consciousness and does not signify that you are.

Deep introspection reveals no substantially existing self that is an independent entity immune form change. The atman or divine spark residing in the heart, the source of the sense of being an entity, does not substantially exist. It is a temporary phenomena and it grows and gathers.

Awareness does not perceive, it has consciousness for that.

Because Awareness is, there is perception but it is a function of consciousness and dependant on there being one that perceives.

Awareness is equally present everywhere, always, already.

If we think of a cinema screen the movies are projected upon it and the screen is equally present and so the projection appears as coherent.The screen was there before the movie began, remained the same all the way through and will remain after it ends. Nothing projected on the screen has any effect on the screen itself.

Consciousness fluctuates and changes sometimes disappearing altogether.

When we sleep there is no consciousness, no sense of "i". We can alter our consciousness states by taking various substances into our body and by various activities. There are no states of awareness it is one.

Awareness is one consciousness is two subject/object.

Consciousness is of something, from something to something but awareness is one self cognising mass.

The Nature of awareness is all around us and it's glory is inconceivable.

The Nature reflects the wondrous nature of awareness which it is an expression of. Attending to Nature can bring us to awareness.

If consciousness meets awareness it becomes pure and it's job is done.

When finally after directing our consciousness to every possible thing we direct it to awareness then the realisation of what is and who we are dawns and consciousness merges back into awareness.

Meditation

The more shallow the breathing the greater the sense of timelessness.

The breathless, deathless, thoughtless place of the eternal stillness is approached by diminishing breath until we come to a complete stand still.Physical stillness and mental quietude make the breath become shallow and the sense of timelessness unfolds.

When the breath is witnessed and there is no interference it will become more and more shallow until it's divine motivating principle is revealed.

The source of breath, thought and the sense' I am' is deep within the Heart follow either back to find it. Liberation is remaining in the Heart. To watch your breath without breathing it is to quiet the mind and gain the greatest sense of being.

Breathlessness is effortless and automatic to one who has collapsed the attention into the heart.

Yogis attempt breath retention by using locks and techniques this brings a completely different result from having your breath naturally approach the breathless, deathless and thoughtless place of the heart.

Effort is important until it is realised that effort and result both happen in unchanging awareness which you are. Then effort is effortless.

At the core there is always the perfect meditation of the natural state, no effort required to generate that state. The cessation of all action is all that's needed just to be present to what really is behind all states of consciousness and everything else.

Bodily sensations exist in a band width of experience, if you find it and then discount it. Now where are you housed?

It's sensations that give us the very convincing idea that we are the body but when we discount that bandwidth of sensation then instantly we are everywhere boundless, formless, vast as the sky.

Have you noticed how in meditation you experience the state, feel the energy move, practice the technique but who are you?

Until one realises the witness Self one is trying to generate and manipulate various mental states thinking that one is better or more relevant than another. However the Witness is prior to them all and is the portal to Awareness.

Knowing experientially, this is Liberation.

Without direct experience of the Self there will be no transformation and consequently no Liberation. Understanding the teachings of Liberation will not bring Liberation it is only by direct cognition that realisation occurs.

There is a difference between peace of mind and the deep silence of the heart.

Peace of mind is a mental state and can be attained by many techniques but does not liberate or yield authentic realisation. Liberation comes with the recognition of the Self as Awareness, unassociated and undivided.

Kundalini energy arriving in the crown chakra, opening the 1000 petals, accessing higher realms is not Self realisation.

Whatever happens takes place in unchanging awareness.You are that.Recognising that brings a profound, lasting transformation to the way that life occurs.One may have a profound experience of inner energies rising and afterwards be exactly the same. This is also true of experiences generated by "medicine'.

Practicing meditation is using techniques meditating is simply being what is.

Practice is a preparation for real meditation which is entirely natural. Techniques become redundant as the Self is recognised. The natural state is the perfect mediation that yields insight and realisation.

In deep stillness the point of view of the observer dissolves and duality ends, only self cognising Awareness remains.

Eventually after being the witness even of meditation states, in deep stillness having returned into the heart cave the duality of subject and object dissolves and all there remains is self cognising awareness.The sheer brilliance of suchness experiencing itself without any observation.

Surrender

Surrendering means putting down all that can be put down in any moment, arriving at the natural state of perfect being.

What seemed impossible becomes possible and even a simple thing to do. In a moment one can cease to identify as the part one is playing with all it's baggage and surrender into what is.

Surrendering ones' point of view, the scope of knowing becomes infinite. Surrendering the psychological self the witness appears, surrendering the witness and there is boundless self cognising awareness.

The more we let go of that which implies a separate self the greater our perception of reality becomes until we get we are that.

Surrendering the psychological self means realising that things don't have to be resolved, you can just put them down.

There are those who think that emancipation and happiness are gained by resolving all the issues of the psychological self but although some issues need to be consciously processed the greater part gets resolved naturally as the Self emerges.

Surrendering means completely accepting things as they are and giving up that they should be other than they are.

We tend to think that we are unhappy because of circumstances internally or externally but insight shows us that its who we are being that circumstances are that determines how they turn up for us and that altering them makes only a temporary and superficial difference.

The Atman

The atman is usually housed in the heart as the shining principle that stimulates breath and originates thinking.

The sense of being an entity distinct from other beings arises from the atman, a self effulgent lit particle that stimulates life, breath and thought.

Sometimes during the lifetime and always at the end of the life the atman travels out through one of the chakric portals.

The atman is a great mystery it is the source of presence, the most essential part of a being. It has no substantial existence and is continuously changing having no fixed or static aspects.

After death a lifetimes' presence energy is reabsorbed into the atman. So one may leave with more than one arrived with.

Some say we come into this world with nothing and leave with nothing but this is not so with the correct instruction we can gather light and presence and when we leave it becomes absorbed into the atman.

The atman body appears as a sphere, the paramatman body is skylike.The param atman is like the dreamer of all dreams, the atman is the dreamer of my dream.

My experience revealed the atman as a lit shining particle at the centre of a sphere. The atman is the soul and the paramatman is the super soul or over soul and Brahman is the substratum of all structures and appearances.

The atman is seen as an object until one becomes it by returning to the source of attention, breath and thought.

This is the goal to return from the adventure of consciousness and become reabsorbed as the atman, leaving behind all sense of identity.

The atman streams light is self effulgent, nothing fires this brilliance. The atman is within a sphere of its own domain.

The atman takes in and gives out simultaneously and is a mystery and great wonder. There is in my experience and aspect of the atman that exists as a sphere in a timeless domain.

Who am I?

Who you are being that you are gives you how you get yourself.

There is no way that you are yet you do appear as if there is and that appearance is given by who you are being that you are.

The wounded child is not a real thing it's a construct which conflates unresolved issues within the psychological self.

Some people relate to this construct almost as if there is a little child within and they go and talk to it, which is fine for some but realisation comes when we let go of our identification with the psychological self and its contents.

Who the past says I Am is not who I Am. The part I have played in the drama of life is not who I am. There is no possibility of who I am being wounded by anything that ever happened.

This is a wonderful thing to realise that the witness is never effected in any way by what it sees. There is a part of us that no trauma ever reached.

Who I think I am is the psychological self, it's a construct and not who I actually am. There is no fixing it, no one ever did, so just put it down.

When you asked your mind who am I? The answer it gave was who you think you are.However fortunately that is not who you are, you prior to it.The witness.

As long as you believe you are not good enough you won't be and nothing will work. However it is just an erroneous idea.

Ideas that are held and nurtured for a longtime have the habit of turning up as drama proving them right.

States of consciousness, thoughts, emotions and drama in your life,doesn't it all just arise?

You don't create the states or think the thoughts do you? For whom does it all arise? Get this and you are freedom itself. Everything has been given but who receives?

Who one thinks one is, who others say one is, who the past says you are, you are none of these.

The character that your thoughts, opinions and actions signify is not you either.Deeper than all this is the witness.

Even when you feel broken, no good and damaged by life, this is seen by a deeper you, one unsullied by events and thoughts, pure and full of love.

This truth is just so wonderful it shows that essentially you are fine.

The historical you is not who you are, who the past says you are is not you.You are unchanging awareness.

You are only, always the presence, no time passes for that one, knowing no age, birth or death you live untouched by all that happens.

The "I" in "I am" does not signify a person but a dynamic of consciousness concentration.

Like a swirl in the Ganga, it arises and passes.The Noble Buddha is said "just because you have the sense 'I am" does not mean that you are!

Taking things personally leads to no end of tedious conversations with yourself.

The Persona is invented and maintained by internal dialogue only. Without the memory of all the conclusions you have come to about life and yourself where would you be? Freedom itself!

Thinking you know best but offering no evidence. You isolate yourself so as not to have to bear any contradiction.

A consequence of identifying as ego is often isolation. Also cult members thinking erroneously they have found the only way tend to only hang out with fellow believers they don't want to be confronted.

Identifying as kind and spiritual is not the same as being kind and spiritual.

The ego/mind has its own version of kindness which tends to be a kind of virtue signalling with the aim of winning people admiration and validation. Acting spiritual is just that, acting.

It is important to be able to distinguish the mind from Self.

The mind talks to itself, the Self is silent knowing, observing the minds machinations and everything else.

The story you tell about your life and the past is just that, a fiction.

The story teller has an agenda and cannot be trusted as a reliable witness. There is no way that it was, it all depends on perspective.

It is true you can't change the past but you can transform the meaning you gave it.

People live in regret thinking what's done is done but the events are over and all that remains is what we made them mean and that we can transform compassionately.

Constantly entertaining internal chatter and commentary you have come to identify as the thinker.

This is the basic cause of suffering. Who listens to you think?

It is so..

If you focus on the pointer and not what is pointed to then you miss the point. Unless of course you see that the pointer is what he is pointing to!

The danger is that people give up the enquiry into 'who am I?' and fall at the gurus feet thinking knowing and being validated by him is the solution and a pseudo devotion can take over from authentic introspection and realisation stops and years pass.

Knowing and being able to extrapolate on the wisdom of the saints is not the same as having it.

The ego mind has this view I understand so I must be enlightened but there is a big difference between understanding and realisation.

As soon as you think you know you leave the path of realisation. As soon as you say "I did it "it stops.

Everything is given and just arises in the being saying "I know" is what the ego/mind does and it then assumes the false identity of a knower. Saying "I did it" cuts off the flow of what actually did do it!

That which measures progress and offers internal commentary has no idea. With truth its always all or nothing.

The valuator,the characteriser,the commentator always is coming from some agenda and cannot be trusted.Truth is not relative.

The nondual view sees only what is and does not divide the world into two.

When there are no filters, agendas or preferences one sees everything as self evident.

No one experiences the natural state, some people experience and attain yogic states which are witnessed.

It is sometimes called the stateless state and cannot be objectified or reified or measured.Certain methods of yogis generate different kinds of states and powers but these are witnessed too.

The distance between you and liberation is given by how far away you are being that it is!

Many believe that their liberation is in some other

life but the truth is there is no actual distance in time between you and it.The liberated space is with you right now and always, it might be today you allow this to be your reality.

For something to be real it must be born of something real. The unreal cannot create the real.

For something to be real it must not change, evolve or have constituent parts.

For something to be real it must have clearly defined edges not made of molecules.

For something to be real it must be seen the same way by all always.

For something to be real it must exist of its own accord completely independent of anything else.

If your happiness is created by circumstances it will not last because all circumstances are constantly changing.

The fact that circumstantially derived happiness does not last is one of the reasons why Buddha said life is suffering.

The happiness does not arise from the circumstances but from who you are being that they are. You are the source of your happiness.

Circumstances do not emanate feelings, one person sees another's death as miserable and another sees the same death as great, showing that we are the source of whatever feelings arise from circumstances.

This life is like a dream in the sense that it seems to be real but is not. Awakening from a sleep dream one realises all of it was equally unreal.

One also realises that the dream was one thing, no element was independent and no element had any substantiality to it even though it seemed to exactly like the appearances in the waking state.

Can you confirm that the main agenda of the persona is looking good to self and others at all times?

This is a shocking realisation when it comes, just how much of our self and behaviours are motivated by this need to validate and perpetuate the current version of ourselves.

Virtue signalling is not the same as being devoted or spiritual. It's an act covering an in authenticity.

Until the Self is realised then we mostly act spiritual thinking somehow this is what spiritual is but nothing except a little admiration comes from being this way.'Spiritual' is not a set of behaviours.

An object appears as a waveform but when observed changes into particular presence.

You are playing a part until you self observe then

you become presence.This is a truth from Quantum physics that describes the human condition exactly.

A Self realised person would tend not to negate others or think that his way is the only way.

Because he knows that who he is being that things are gives him how he get's them and that phenomena have no fixed or real identity.

Being in presence exposes what one would rather not accept about oneself, selfishness, judgementalness and other unseemly aspects.

Eventually one exhibits the qualities of presence, joy, kindness humility and love.

There is no way that life is except the one that confirms who you are being that it is.

Life occurs uniquely for each being and there is no way that it is.

Not everything in this life is rational, logical or explainable.

The benefits of taking a bath in the Ganga or Love are good examples.

Two carnal eyes see what appears to be but is not but the inner eye sees what is both within and without and in every moment.

There is more than one kind of vision and when that inner vision is happening the spectrum of perception expands.

Some people are naturally kind, the rest of us have to work on it

And work on it we must or we will become cantankerous and cynical in our old age.

Understanding is of the intellect and opens the possibility of realization which is direct experience of what is prior to thought.

There is a distinction between understanding and realization.What the intellect knows and deduces can be lost and forgotten but what is realised by direct experience becomes who you are.

The intellect is eventually surpassed as the lover of truth enters the field of pure undifferentiated wisdom.

In that place no thoughts pass as there is only awakeness.Wisdom is direct experience of what is, all concepts and notions are redundant.

A loving relationship is quite rare most people are involved in psychological entanglements of one kind or another.

As long as we are identifying as the psychological self or who we think we are then it is most likely we will attract and live out psychologically based relationships. Many confuse psychological entanglement for relationship. Real love causes no pain.

Identifying as spiritual or as a devotee is optional and has nothing to do with self realisation although for some it might appear that way.

What is truly is spiritual is flowing as the Self, acting spiritual and virtue signalling is just trying to get people to validate your new version of yourself.

When sleep dreaming, the dreamer, the dreaming and the contents of the dream are one and the same.

It is the same upon awakening. Are we dreaming we are awake or awake dreaming?

If you want to save a moment be fully present in it. This is a secret teaching of the Awakened ones.

At the end of life in the place of integration after death what was experienced as a dream fades into oblivion but moments of presence of saved. Few know this truth.

The psychological self is not who we are but who we think we are.

We ignore what is confronting and accentuate what is good about us and project that into the world as us hoping others will believe it. We range from thinking we are somehow broken to thinking we are special!

First humility then greatness.

Everyone has the possibility of greatness which is

not a quality of ego but the consequence of moving as the Self.

Knowledge is distinct from Knowingness.

There is knowledge of something but knowingness is the feeling of being in omni science and is direct experience unsupported by concepts or thought.

Those who seek just for themselves get off to a good start but soon fall away.

Those with even a little altruistic intent to their seeking get all the help they need, those who are practising to generate happiness and peace for themselves tend to fall away.

The seeker becomes the finder who dissolves in the finding.

After finding no one remains. The ego never finds. The studier never realises.

The minor mysteries are manifold but the major mystery is one.

Beings can spend lifetimes wondering in the mystery maze until finally the Awareness is realised. The greatest mystery is Love, minor mysteries are reincarnation, karma, siddhi powers, kundalini, chakras etc.

The price of completion is forgiveness of yourself and all others.

Knowing that if you had experienced their causes and conditions you would have done exactly the same.

Acts of random kindness are powerful.

If you do something genuinely kind with no hidden agenda to benefit yourself, you will find that your gesture has extraordinary results. Kindness is the antidote to the toxicity of self cherishing selfishness. Selflessness is the quality of one being run by love.

Karma does not exist, it is not a thing.

It is a designation given to apparent links between one thing happening and another.It is a conceptual superimposition on inconceivable causality.

There is no such thing as 'God testing me'.

This is a man made designation which tries to give meaning to events which actually have none.

The core of every state is the same.

All the waking states, dream states and deep sleep happen in unchanging Awareness. Those who don't know this from direct experience are still dreaming they are awake.

No one state of consciousness is any more real than any other.

They all begin and end and have their being in Awareness.A high state of consciousness is no more than a low state and reality is equidistant to them both.

The feeling of life is the only real thing there is.

Everything else exists as insubstantial appearance only.Just like how the objects appearing in a sleep dream are seen to have no real existence upon awakening.

Rejoin the global ecosystem energetically, experientially and actually.

We do this by coming into the Presence of what is now and seeing how it is boundless and all pervading.The entire creation is in this now vibrating life.We are not separate from it we are part of it.

Once we start to stabilise as this Presence the illusion is naturally exposed and transcended.

The illusion is what seemed to be real but is not.

Magick only works when conjured from the level of Gnosis.

The manipulation of energies and circumstances can only happen when the illusion is clearly seen.

New gifts,powers and extraordinary capabilities arise naturally upon awakening.

Choices can reconfigure how Presence expresses through a being.

Keep softening your heart melting into what is until you find the Self as a field of Love.

Perhaps the greatest secret of all is that The Unified Filed is love, love unconditional and Universal.

Behind the field of atoms and particles is what?

At the moment after the Big Bang space unfolded into what? Can you see where space is housed? Space is not Reality.

The opened third eye can see where space is housed; particles dancing inside and out.

It sees the luminosity that is the ground of being and it sees all the lights.This view shows that the seer, the seeing and the seen are one and the same.

The third eye can generate a beam of attention that focuses light particles.

It can be focused on inner points or outer ones. Immediately upon paying attention one becomes present.Extraordinary powers or siddhis are said to manifest when this beam of attention is placed on different objects.

Becoming present means by self observation to collapse the waveform and come into particle presence consciously.

There are two modes of appearance as a waveform or as particle presence this is what Quantum reality suggests and the mystic knows directly, as soon as one self observes presence unfolds and there is peace,clarity and the luminosity that is the ground of being shines forth.

When one sits still and softens the heart each breath can be experienced as a blessing of love. Happening to a lover in a field of love.

This is the ultimate position for a human, the point where the unified field of energy is felt as unconditional love, the breath itself is love all around is love!

How to open a moment.

Choose to stop thinking for a moment let everything be just exactly as it is, do nothing don't manipulate consciousness, don't practice any technique just let be what is. As soon as you drop in a moment opened.The moment remains open as long as you are present in it. Into the open moment the truth rushes peace becomes more and more blatant, joy and clarity unfold.

Most people spend their whole lives trying to improve their circumstances. The wise one develops immunity to circumstance and gains a stable happiness from within.

That immunity is developed by realising that the circumstances are empty and emanate nothing, who I am being that they are gives me how I get them.

When, for a moment we drop everything that we cling to we float without form weightless in the now.

This is the sweetest freedom and the realisation that the psychological self can simply be put down is life changing.

Let everything be to the point where you stop inventing meanings and narratives.

This is the beautiful simplicity. This is the great challenge to let life speak for itself and stop interpreting and inventing stories.

When you are not there you can see things and people as they are.When you are there your vision is corrupted by your ideas, preconceptions and other biases.

Every action reaches perfection when you are not there interfering but simply observing, this includes seeing things as they are.

Get over yourself by realising there is no way that you are.

So much anxiety created by trying to figure out how and who we are and then it dawns 'there is no way we are!"The only place you actually exist is now and if you look now you will see there is no way that you are. You are a clearing for all appearance.

Don't wait for your ideal set of circumstances to turn up before you allow yourself to be happy.

The truth is you can be happy whilst standing in deep sh.t!

You are responsible for how you get others. I am not responsible for how you get me.

As there is no way that others are how you get them is given by who you are being that they are and your responsibility.

Chapter 2

Stages On The Path

Stage One: There must be something more.

Entry onto the path very often it's preceded with the sense that there must be something more. Feeling of being incomplete and that something is not quite right but what that is is very hard to define with words. It's as if there is a thirst that has arisen from a deep place within where none of the normal past times and pursuits seem to quite do it. Or an itch that just cannot be scratched by life in the normal sense.

Plato used a word entelechy. Entelechy is the thirst to know, like a deeply embedded program in the core of our being we know that we can know and we feel called to know. Even just accepting this feeling of a thirst for knowledge is there can activate a set of circumstances that lead ultimately to its quenching.

Many people at this stage when they haven't quite got on the Path experience all kinds of synchronicities, meaningful dreams, signs and intuitions pointing to the Path and confirming that yes there is something more and we must pursue it as a matter of some urgency.

Stage Two: Getting on the Path

The next stage, typically as we feel the thirst for something more, the way to fulfil that thirst synchronistically and magically appears in our life. Perhaps it's a teacher or a master or a practice or a community.

Many people try out all kinds of different methods and practices some people take medicine like Ayauaska, San Pedro or Kambo and have profound awakening experiences doing so. Others may engage in different kinds of meditation practices to see if it suits them.

As soon as possible it is recommended to find your method, your practice, your teacher and to commit to that in earnest and make the experience of peace your number one priority in your life.

At this time people become initiated or take

some sacred vows or in a deep moment of cognition commit to a life of self enquiry and service. This amounts to getting on the Path. Now you have direction, now you have your method, now the way opens up in front of you and the destination is clear. The destination is your liberation from suffering.

I have noticed that many people reach this stage and start a practice and in the beginning their experience is inspired and there are transforming realisations. However further down the path they either leave it or the flow of realisation becomes dried up and their practice becomes a habit and the fruit is not enjoyed in quite the same way it was at the beginning and then eventually they fall away.

Then there are those who get on the Path maintain their practice and find that whenever they need it, help appears and guides them, whether it be insights they need to have arising from within, or help and Grace from enlightened beings. Whatever they might need to maintain their trajectory on the Path towards liberation appears for them.

What is the difference between the two types of people? I have noticed that the ones who maintain the journey on the Path to truth have an altruistic aspect in their intention and aspiration. They want to become free so that they may free others, they want to become clear that they may help others. These are the ones whose progress is blessed and unstoppable. Those who practice to generate happiness for themselves and to seek their own liberation generally fall away because that kind of intention is not strong enough and is ultimately selfish.

It is definitely a stage on the path when you find in your Heart a small space where there is an authentic caring about the well-being of others. As one walks on the Path that small space can grow and grow until the compassion that so many write about, is actually felt in your own heart.

Stage Three: Who am I?

There is a stage on the path before it has become clear who I truly am, where I identify as 'spiritual' and in so doing I measure myself against others, who is more spiritual? This is a very dangerous time although it doesn't necessarily appear that it is, everything may be going very well, I may be having my service doing my practice and having experiences but I am very pleased with myself and conceit and pride can develop.

Conceit and spiritual pride is very hard to root out and that is why being in the presence of people generating a high vibration is very important because that vibration acts like a bright mirror bringing to light these subtle defilements and obstructions.

I am not the thinker!

Another important stage on the path is when one realises that 'I am not the thinker'. Identifying as the thinker keeps us locked in a barren world. Identifying as the mind we have a life experience where there is minimal love, joy and no peace. What joy and love there is arises at the direction of the internal dialogue that evaluates everything and orders our appropriate emotional response. We don't realise how it is, our thoughts arise we think they are a direct response and reflection of reality and so we believe them and allow them to construct our identity and the reality from which we live.

All of our suffering comes through one portal and that is the portal of thought. Even physical pain can be seen just as a sensation but it is thought that turns that physical sensation into suffering.

There comes a point in deep meditation where one can objectify the thinking process and see that actually thoughts arise of their own accord given by who we are being in any one moment. Extracting oneself from identifying as the thinker is the ꞙginning of real and lasting liberation and as such important stage on the Path.

ꞓr way of arriving at this conclusion that ꞑe thinker is to recognise the fact that if ꞇhinker you would be able to tell yourself to be quiet and your mind and your thoughts would go quiet. But even if you tell yourself to be still and quiet your mind still rumbles on. This means that something else apart from your will is driving the thinking process.

Looking more closely we begin to recognise that we think in different voices sometimes perhaps the voice of our father or the voice of fear or the voice of a teacher's disapproval or the voice of confidence.

Which of these voices is ours? The answer to that question is none of them.Sometimes our thinking gets out of control and affects our sleep and we become mentally destabilised by galloping thoughts. When that is happening our thinking consumes us and we lose perspective and collapse into a mentally based reality.The only way that I have found to still the mind is to distinguish yourself as the listener, the one who hears those thoughts, you wouldn't know you were thinking unless something was hearing them. The thinker and the one who hears the thoughts are distinct and different from each other.

Peace, salvation, liberation, happiness and a sense of purpose are not going to be found in the mental world,the realm of thoughts and thinking. As the great freedom and spaciousness of awareness unfolds for you you realise that living in a mentally based reality believing you were the thinker and having your reality made up of endless internal dialogue was in fact similar to living in a hell realm.

At this stage on the path it feels like a breakthrough has been made and now the student knows that it is possible to pull away from the gravity of a mentally based reality and to move into the joy of pure presence.

Stage four: Presence

When we identify as the thinker and live in reality supported by internal dialogue, we don't have a sense of presence we never actually make it fully into the here and now. We are always just outside thinking about the past and the future trapped in a mentally based reality.

By some grace, that energy that makes what seemed impossible possible, we get a sense of what presence is. Living in our minds believing ourselves to be the thinker we never get to experience our presence in this here now.

Quantum scientists tell us that matter manifests in one of two ways at its most basic level either it is a waveform or it appears as particle presence. Amazingly what creates the difference is observation. It is the same with us we travel through life as a waveform travelling from birth to death but if we self observe we have the experience of breaking down into particle presence. At this point our sense of density dissolves, a sense of solidity and weight dissolves and we perceive ourselves as an energetic mass vibrating in the now.

When we manifest as pure presence we are whole, complete and fulfilled and at peace. When we are in presence we emanate, radiate and vibrate. When we manifest as presence our individual energy field merges with the total energy field of all life and we realise that we are a part of this fantastic ecosystem, the planet Earth, the universe and all life.

Being present is the same as being awake, living in presence is the life of the awakened.

The more time we spend as pure presence, the simpler, calmer and more wonderful life becomes. The presence of life itself heals the heart of obscure unresolved emotions and it heals the mind of misunderstandings and ignorance. Being present to what actually is the whole of the way. One cannot really say what presence, suchness or reality actually is it's unreifiable it's magnificent beyond our capacity to comprehend and convey.

But we can surely experience it and once we have recognised it then it becomes increasingly easy to be. Presence does not fluctuate, it's the same everywhere, always, already. The one place where we can safely surrender, let go and put down our burden is in Presence.

The confidence that arises out of experiencing the self as presence leads us onto the next stage of the unfoldment which is the recognition of the empty and insubstantial nature of everything within the phenomenal world. The world is empty of anything substantial but it is full of presence.

Stage five: Emptiness

A very important stage on the path is when we come to realise the empty nature of the phenomenal world and all the structures in it. Along with this we realise that there is no inherent meaning to life that it is empty and meaningless. But in a good way!

Most people read and receive teachings about emptiness before they realise that it is actually so. For the unprepared mind the realisation that life is empty and meaningless can be quite shocking because it can be mistaken to mean that there is nothing.

If you dream of somebody in the dream they appear to have meaning they appear to emanate life and be independent. When we wake up we realise that they had no independent existence and the meaning we experienced of them in the dream, we gave them that meaning.

In our lives we do experience things as having meaning and circumstances as having purpose. What we often fail to recognise is that we are the ones assigning that meaning and purpose. For example let's say somebody dies- to the one who loved the departed it's a matter of great misery but to the person who didn't know the departed it means nothing at all. If the death had any intrinsic meaning everyone would get it equally but the event of that persons passing has no emanation or meaning that is universal, how people get it is up to them.

When we consciously stop projecting meaning into life and let it be what ever it actually is we see that it is empty but strangely the emptiness is filled by wonderful presence.

Emptiness means that nothing exists independently from anything else, everything relies on everything else for existence, nothing exists completely independently of everything else.

Recognising emptiness is to see that essentially everything is the same and made of the same substance. In exactly the same way as the contents of a sleep dream are also made of the same substance. When we're in the dream it seems like the diamond is hard and space is not filled with anything when we wake we know that there was nothing substantial about any element of the dream.By deeply relaxing we can come to a place where, wonderfully, we recognise the dream like and empty nature of the waking state and all that is in it. When life is seen as empty and meaningless it follows that it is without purpose there is no purpose that emanates from anything. As conscious beings we get to choose and create our own purpose and this defines who we are in the drama.

When we disengage from the world, when we disassociate from our thoughts and our memories and meanings, when we let go of all that we think life is and we are, then the possibility of recognising the emptiness that is so full of presence can open up for us. When we see that so much of what we thought was important and meaningful really isn't and that what is truly important is to be present, for as much of our time as possible, to the truth of what is. Suchness, the pure presence of life itself, this is coming home, this is waking up.

Chapter 3

The Psychological Self

Many people think 'I am my behaviours and I must research my psychology, my unconscious mind and find out why my behaviours are like they are and then that will tell me who I am and then my existential identity crisis finally comes to an end!'.

But this really isn't the case, my characteristics and the content of my unconscious does not reveal who I am, I am not the psychological self. That refers to the unconscious aspects of the part that I've been playing in the drama of my life. It's always changing there is nothing static in the psychological self, looking at it from different perspectives I see it differently. Looking at it from different times I see it differently, there is actually not a core or anything solid to find.

When I inhabit the view 'there is no way that I am' then immediately such joy, spaciousness and freedom unfold for me. There isn't anything fixed about me. Is there a way that the sky is? No, there is no way that the sky is, you cannot describe the sky by telling us it's content just as you can't describe your Self by describing the content of the psychological mind. They are as different as the sky is to the weather. There is no way that the sky is, it has no qualities and it is definitely distinct from the content it holds. The sky does not evolve nor do I. The sky never changes no do I. The sky is boundless and so am I.

There is a Buddhist practice called Sky Gazing and some people think it's about looking at the clouds and projecting onto them shapes and faces. Sky gazing is definitely not looking at the clouds or admiring the blue. Sky gazing is when you become present to what it actually is distinct from it's content. I am the same, what about me never changes? What about me is always present in every situation that I find myself?

People say you must love yourself that's the way to happiness. What is really meant here? I am this sky like awareness and as I become increasingly that, I realise that actually it is love. Beyond any form of personal love, for me or any others, is this incredible unconditional love which I truly am. In the absence of true self knowledge I create a construct that I call myself and that I try to accept and that I try to Love but it's still just a narrative, a story I tell about myself.

When we really look within not just into the chaos of the unconscious mind or the psychological self, we do not find anyone, there is no one there. All there is vast and spacious awareness and that is something that we need to become comfortable with and in so doing we will find a heavy burden of the construct that we call our self will dissolve and fall away and we will awaken as the Self having lost the causes of suffering and gained our freedom.

Many people spend a lot of time and a great deal of money trying to sort out the psychological self. Even if you sort it out will you be any happier? If that was so then the happiest people would be the psychotherapists but clearly that isn't the case! The path to happiness, the way to freedom from suffering is first to distinguish the Self which is prior to the psychological self. To understand what is the observer and who exactly witnesses the different states that come from the varying degrees of confusion within the psychological Self. The one who witnesses the effects of trauma is that one traumatised? The one that witnesses my confusion is that one confused?

Once I establish myself as the observer then I can look at the psychological self from a place that is whole,unassociated and stable. Then it's much easier to accept needs to be accepted aboutthe past, to release pent-up emotion and become resolved.

Trying to sort out the psychological self whilst still identifying as it, is a fool errand. You cannot fight fire with fire, we need to become separate from the psychological self, turn it into an object that can be viewed dispassionately and then insights occur and progress in resolving and feeling the past is much quicker.

Many people are running a program that says 'I'm not good enough'. If we are not good enough then nothing works, relationships don't work, prosperity isn't there because we are simply not good enough to succeed at anything. A root negative thought most likely created early on in a time of trauma, has a powerful effect on the way we experience virtually all aspects of our life. So it is imperative that before any real healing can happen on the psychological level we first establish our self as the Self which is whole and not supported by thoughts of any kind.

This is the optimum viewing point from which to resolve and release the issues of the past.

Another thing people do to suppress the dysfunctions of the psychological self is to take medications, drugs, alcohol and this does work in the short term but it is costly. Medication seems to numb the frequencies of pain and disturbance but it also robs us of the higher subtle frequencies So we end up zombified, existing but not really experiencing any passion or pleasure.

If we are using marijuana, hashish etc. then we have a blissful state and then when the drugs finish very often people notice that anger has arisen when you can't get your next bag one becomes angry and irritable. It's in the irritation that you see just how much you had been suppressing and perhaps unknowingly using the drugs to suppress your unresolved feelings from the past. So everything that we use to avoid our dysfunctions has a cost, either a cost physically or a cost to our capacity to perceive the subtleties of this life and a financial cost.

However there are times when medication is absolutely essential. Extreme mental states very often do call for extreme measures but it's never ideal.

Bonfire of the Vanities

Is there anything more important or that influences our behaviour more than wanting to look good to ourselves and others at all times.? Every kind of action and interpretation is infected by this need to feel good about ourselves as personalities and have others agree with who we currently think we are.I was judging a lover for spending so much time putting on makeup, "vanity, vanity" I thought. Then I decided to look it up and what I found confronted me "'it flattered his vanity to think I was in love with him" ouch! It so did! and then "she had none of the vanity so often associated with beautiful women". Ok.doubleouch! I had defined vanity so that it did not apply to me!

Other words for Vanity are conceit, conceitedness, self-conceit, narcissism, self-love, self-admiration, self-regard,self-absorption,self-obsession,self-centredness, egotism, egoism, egocentrism, egomania; pride, haughtiness, arrogance, boastfulness, swagger, imperiousness, cockiness, pretension, affectation, airs, show, ostentation;

It seems that everyone thinks there is something

wrong with them and it's balanced by thinking that they are special. This specialness may or may not ever actually show up in real life.

How would life be if I was not concerned with looking good to myself and others at all the time? I would be authentic doing things in the way they should be done not using things as a vehicle for looking good. Living as an ego contaminates literally everything.

The truth about most of humanity is that we are suffering under a perpetual existential identity crisis,we simply do not know who we are so we keep on inventing new versions of our selves and judge their effectiveness by how well others believe our projections. It's easy to see in others not so easy to detect in our selves because if we saw our inauthenticity, our vanity, we would not look good to ourselves. So we take great efforts to only see what confirms who we get ourselves to be.

The good news is that this Psychological self, who the mind says we are, the source of our manias, vanities and ego, can actually just be put down, even if it's just for a moment to start with, it can be put down. It's like a hat we have been wearing and we have been subjected to the effect of it when we just take it off it turns into an object that can be examined and seen for what it is.Then the question comes when I put my psychological self down what is left? What does it feel like? Its spacious, clear, peaceful and awake. If I do this again in 10 minutes it will be exactly the same, it never changes. From this putting down arises a new sense of self. This Self is a being not a mental construct it is whole and wonderful in every case.

When the ego is seen it falls away and the shining Self emerges as the simple sense I AM.

The Myth of the Within

The within was a place to take refuge in, made of fabricated habitual consciousness states where some peace could be felt. Not the deep unmoving peace of reality but a little relative peace of mind. It's like watching movies, its somewhere to go hide out so I can keep being dulled to the reality of existence.

The myth is taught that this little cave within is where the truth is and if you just sit in it everyday salvation is assured and that light you see that means you are enlightened and those frequencies are actually divine music of the spheres all of this means you are having a special experience that is truly spiritual and because of that you get 'special" status for being in the know.

However no Liberation comes this way no matter how long you sit in that cave.It does not dissolve the ego/ self rather it perpetuates it. That kind of activity does not dissolve deep rooted anger, addictions or wounds of trauma, it makes no difference at all. It makes me feel rested for a bit and superior indefinitely.

Beliefs have the effect of decorating the inner cave and generally the stronger the belief the more alienated from reality we become until we can only really relate to those who share the same beliefs.

So now life within starts to become a cause for dysfunction. Many of those who believe in 'within' only want it for the refuge it brings, a little peace and protection for the ego/self and that is what they get. What locks us in illusion is the idea of being a body and the thinker, the truth of our true nature can be quite shocking that is why it's best to realise it now rather than later at the time of death.

It is often said that the truth is within and peace is within and for salvation all one needs is to turn within. I believed this for a long time. Now I see differently one can develop cosy states that give shelter from the storm and chaos of life but there is no inner mystical state that leads to liberation more than any other, one can spend decades staring at inner light and not get any closer to liberation.

Developing comfortable states of consciousness through meditation or anything else is not an approach to Liberation. How very shocking this is! All that these practises and beliefs do is divert us from the sheer terror of our ignorance and mortality, our true position, how life actually is.

There is the possibility of Liberation where the dualism of within and without becomes utterly flattened and consciousness states and trying to generate and manipulate them becomes irrelevant. Liberation comes when terror blasts us out of complacency and the ego realm of state development and consciousness control. Liberation does not happen to anybody it happens when the Self and all its ordinary and extraordinary refuges are transcended.

This maybe at the time of death when the shocking reality of how things actually are can no longer be avoided or anesthetised by manipulating our experience in one way or another. Or it may come like it did for Ramana Maharshi, out of the blue.

One day he became completely terrified by the idea of his death this deep contracting blasted him out of his ego self nurturing into absolute self cognising awareness.

For me my terror came when I had a near death experience. A great wind arose within me and blasted me out of my body consciousness, it was completely beyond my control and very frightening but then I looked up and saw the proverbial light at the end of the tunnel. I was about to make my way to it when I felt to slow down and look around as I did I saw that everything that I had ever or would ever be or experience was happening in unchanging awareness and I am that, at that moment a voice behind me said'that is why you meditated'. To be able to remain calm enough to see what is. Then my friend called me back and I returned.To be born again we must die.

I am my Gender?

Some years ago a man came to see me with an unusual question on his mind. He wanted to know whether he should have a sex change operation or not. This was the first time that I had encountered someone considering this option in their lives.

I asked him why he wanted to do that and he replied that he had never really felt that he was who he was. He never really felt comfortable in his identity as a man and that he felt sure that if he went through the long process of transforming himself into a woman this would remove his deep feeling of unease about who he was.

He said he felt that he could never really be fully himself and that he was never really fully happy. It was like having an itch that could not be scratched.

After some years he came back to see me and he was indeed transformed into a very lovely woman his voice had changed his body had changed, his face had changed and he seemed happy. I asked him about his journey and the results that it had brought him. She said that she had had a profound insight after she had all this treatment and surgery.

She said that she had realised that she was looking for her identity in the realm of gender but now she had realised that her true identity was deeper than her gender. Nevertheless she said there was an issue that had been solved by her change of gender and that she was happy with it.

I think everybody goes through a period of having an existential identity crisis, it's a time where we choose an identity and we question our identity and we address the feeling of unease that comes from not really knowing who we are. Perhaps it's triggered by thinking that everybody else seems so sure of who they are and we ourselves feel insecure and not confident in who we are.

Gender only refers to the characteristics of women, men, girls and boys that are socially constructed.This includes norms, behaviours and roles associated with being a woman, man, girl or boy, as well as relationships with each other. As a social construct, gender varies from society to society and can change over time.

Within our body is the soul and the soul does not have a gender. There are not female souls and male souls. I have seen my past lives and they have been female and male ones.

If a person thinks that the way to remedy the existential identity crisis is to change their gender it is unlikely that doing that will have the desired affect.These days there are many who do identify as their gender and the gender options have increased including male, female, transgender, gender neutral, non-binary, agender, pangender, genderqueer, two- spirit, third gender, and all, none or a combination of these. There are many more gender identities then I have listed.But is that really who I am or is it the part I am playing?

The sense of disease that comes from not knowing who you are is there by design and serves a very important purpose, which is to put us on the path to find the answer to the question who am I? Many people think that they are the behaviours they exhibit and the thoughts that they think and the feelings that they have or the preferences that they have. Or perhaps they think they are their gender. But who we are is none of these things, these things refer to the character that we play in the drama of life and we have a deeper identity than this and it is only in finding this deeper identity that the identity crisis gives way to a deep joy of being finally who we actually are.

My point is that people should change their gender if they feel to do that, how wonderful, my point is if it's arising out of an identity crisis and the idea is that the reason I'm not happy is because I should be a woman and that's really who I am, there is actually a deeper truth than that - being the true Self, which has no qualities or characteristics. This will dissolve the crisis of identity.

If a young person wants to engage in therapies to change their sex I would suggest to first establish who you are essentially, as a being, as the Self. The part of you that will not change ever, know this first then you can be sure that your choices are informed and that you are not being motivated by unconscious agendas.

The Self that is the root of our being has no characteristics and remains unassociated with all that happens. Which means that it cannot be traumatised or damaged or hurt by anything that happens in the drama of our life.

The idea that we are who we think we are is a very difficult notion to go beyond. As long as we think that we are who we think we are then we will suffer identifying in that way. However when we realise the Self, the true Self, then there is a great relief, confidence and peace of mind.

What is the ego?

The ego is the false idea of the self, it's an idea, it's a construct developed when we asked our mind who am I? In Indian ashrams and in other places, they have this 'smash the ego' thing and it really doesn't work and it's really not necessary. I was in an ashram and there was service to do. I thought I will clean the toilets. So I cleaned the toilets and that also included cleaning up bird pooh so that the guru wouldn't have to walk on it. I did that for three seasons and it's so funny because you think this is going to be really humbling, I'm going to be really humbled! But the ego can take credit or can make something out of anything! So the next thing I'm feeling proud that the great me is doing something so menial as cleaning the toilets for everybody else!

The ego can make capital out of anything, it can tell you you're great for doing something and it'll tell you you're terrible for doing something. It values you with everybody else 'oh I'm better than this one, I'm not good enough'. It's maintained by internal dialogue, it's the internal dialogue that evaluates you and tells you how you are relative to everything else. This is life as an ego centric being.

As long as we identify as that then we will suffer.

However great we think we are there'll always be someone greater, who no doubt will turn up at exactly the most inconvenient moment! It never fully works, the ego and it's promises.

Whatever you get from the ego crumbles just as you get it so what to do? The answer is simple to recognise that there's something beyond the ego there's another 'I' there's a deeper 'I', there's the 'I' that is the'I' of the observer, the 'I' of the witness.

Don't worry about your ego, don't try and do anything, be awake, be aware, watch and have some vigilance about who you're being because who you're being that you are will give you how you get yourself. If who you're being is that 'I am the part I'm playing in the story of my life' that will give you how you get yourself and then you will have to face the consequences.

Just by being vigilant and pursuing the 'I' the true 'I' the'I am",then naturally your relationship and your identification with the ego will diminish and as you awaken more and more you'll be able to see if and when you're being driven by it or not.

It's a subtle thing but as you awaken your discernment, your ability to see that will increase and then it's a matter of your own integrity. Do you want the fruit of being in your ego which is limited and has consequences or do you want to relinquish that and come into the 'I am'. Now sometimes we don't, sometimes what the ego promises we feel driven to go for.

The great psychologists have said what you're unconscious of drives your life, otherwise we'd all be getting what we consciously want but we don't, why is that? because your unconscious drives your life, your unconscious drives you and we have unconscious desires and compulsions and things that need rebalancing.

You're either being driven by your unconscious or you're consciously driving and to be consciously driving you have to be conscious of that 'I am' and then as you spend less and less time in the unconscious being driven by the past, being driven by all that unresolved psychological stuff then your relationship with it shifts, you pull the energy out of it and of its own accord the ego finds its proper place.

As long as we're in a body in the drama of this life there will be some sense of ego, there will be some sense of the part you're playing and that's fine, the thing is not to be identifying as the part that you're playing.

The ego is not complete so it's always trying to get complete, the ego is not fulfilled, so it's always trying to get fulfilled but this 'I am' presence is fulfilment.

I remember seeing a program where Elton John had just performed to a hundred thousand people his ego was fully adored everyone was chanting his name and then he came off stage and it wasn't enough he said' I can't relate' it wasn't enough, the ego wasn't fulfilled, it hadn't shifted him, hadn't fulfilled him.

One good moment as this 'I am' and a fulfilment immediately starts to unfold, goodness immediately starts to unfold, wholeness immediately starts to unfold.

Coming back into that beautiful place of the observer and that place is full of love, that place is peaceful and clear always. It's not like sometimes it's clear and sometimes it isn't, the observer is always complete clarity it doesn't change.

The ego sometimes is relatively clear but it's always got different agendas bubbling up from different levels, it never knows really quite what it's doing, it blunders and blusters but the 'I am the witness" the deeper one, that one is clarity, that one is freedom and coming from that place is so wonderful.

What the ego promised and could never deliver, the sense I am, the witness immediately blesses us with and we recognise 'I am this'.I was who I thought I was and it caused me suffering, so much pain fluctuating from being not good enough and having it that everybody's better than me, to thinking I was special and better than everybody or any number of a huge range of thoughts that the ego feeds us either to lift us up or to bring us down and keep us in its bondage.

The main thing to understand is that whatever you think the ego is going to bring, it isn't and it doesn't. It takes a lot of effort to pursue the ego's drives but the fruit is never what was offered in the beginning, however pursuing this 'I am', this beautiful place, recognizing the witness, coming from that place, that beautiful simplicity, that real confidence is totally wonderful. The ego offers only bravado which masquerades as confidence.

How to get back to the 'I am'.

There are many methods but there's a very simple method that Ramana Maharshi offered and I have used it a lot. It's amazing and it's so simple if you're ready if you want to move into a deeper place.

So sit still with your with your eyes open and fix them on a point and try not to blink, just keep focused. If your mind is very racy, having your eyes open and fixing them on one point and not blinking that's your intention. That's quite a good way of getting your concentration levels up quickly, it wakes you up immediately, you focus, focus, focus don't move, keep the focus.

If you already are kind of focused then you close your eyes, as you please, but once you've got yourself aligned and settled clarify your intention.

What is your intention? To become this 'I am' presence, to recognize the 'I am' prior to the chattering self. That simple place from which you breathe, from which your thoughts arise from which you view this world, from which you hear this world, from which you witness this world, and experience your mental states.

So the simple way to do it is just to say the word 'I' again and again and notice what happens. You see that by saying it something actually happens.

Do it mentally or out loud and keep going again and again as if the 'I' is a pick ax and you are mining to get through to a seem of gold.

Now if you do this earnestly with full attention and noticing what is happening for even ten minutes a sense of quietening down arises, the sense of coming out of the chattering ego self which is only made of thought and commentary.

The sense of being an individual entity arises in the Heart and by declaring 'I" your attention is pulled out of the mind and tunnels back to the Heart.

Just saying "I" brings your attention back in the direction that you want to be going in and very soon, if not immediately, you feel this incredible sense of 'I am' existence, presence and life.

Resting as that the great wonder starts to unfold of what is the Self and where is the Self and what idsgod. What is the over Self? What is the totality and how does myself relate and connect with that? All that can and must be experienced and realised.

When you experience it and realise it then your relationship to your ego automatically and naturally shifts, your relationship with your life automatically shifts, your relationship to love naturally shifts from being something that you feel to being something that you essentially are. A deep gratitude flows from the heart and sorrow and suffering depart.

After some time of earnest daily practice you awaken to the fact that it's been a long time since you really suffered. It doesn't mean that everything goes right but when things go wrong you have enough awakeness not to suffer about it.

What Ramana Maharshi suggested that for people who are really busy to just go around the whole time as you're doing things mentally repeating 'I' 'I' 'I' and you'll find that your perspective shifts, you'll find that you just start flowing as that 'I am" presence.This technique does not sound like much, it's not glamorous, but if you actually try it you will be surprised at what you feel!

When you really come into that 'I' your breath will come very shallow. The breathless, deathless state and you touch on what wasn't born and won't die about you, you touch on the very core of your being, the very essence of yourself.

Soon you become familiar with the presence of the 'I am' that you are and then you may be able to just find it on a thought or a breath. Living your life as Presence becomes easier and easier.

Also as you progress you recognise the benefits of doing that more and more and you realise that actually you're quite safe to put everything down. You don't have to be carrying your cross to give you a sense of identity any more. When I was in old Jerusalem I came around the corner and there was 10 full-sized crucifixion crosses, all stacked up against a wall with little wheels on the bottom and basically people had hired the crosses for the day and had been walking around carrying their crosses and then at the end of the day they put them up against this wall!

We are like that and the invitation from life is to put your cross down, you're not going to resolve it, just put it down. You don't have to carry it through all of your life, put it down. Be free, be free! By putting it down and recognizing something that's deeper than who you think you are.

When you're in a good mood you think you're great and special and when you're in a bad mood you think you're no good, so which are you? You're neither, you're not who you think you are, you are behind all that internal chatter.The 'I am' presence. This is where the simple technique takes you.

'Who am I?' examine that, inquire into that and these treasures of the 'I am' that you are will open up for you.

Opening Moments

The great meditation, the true meditation will just absorb you anyway and concentrate you naturally but if you want to you can do things that will increase your capacity to concentrate. In Buddhism there's a method called Anapana and that works incredibly well it's very simple and it really is effective if you do it for a while.

The technique is to just place your attention on the space above your top lip below your nose. Your task is just to be present to the sensation of air coming in and coming out through your nostrils and over this area. If you do that for a bit you'll notice that your capacity to focus starts to come together and if you do it a lot then you'll really notice your focus increase.

To start with it's difficult you want to put your attention on your breath or you want to put your attention on a point or just want to sit in the natural state and for a moment you do it and then your mind runs off.

After a while if you persist, you'll be able to place your attention on where you want it to be and have it rest there more and more easily.

The key to realisation is to be able to experience

longer and longer uninterrupted moments. Most of the moments we experience are 10 seconds maximum long between one thought and another.

By not blinking and by not thinking we open a continuous moment, immediately something starts to happen you start to become present to what you weren't aware of that was part of this moment, the energy, the clarity, the peace.

The longer you keep the moment unbroken by not blinking or by not going off in your thoughts the more it unfolds until it becomes increasingly luminous.

The Buddha after his enlightenment under the Bodhi Tree moved from the tree and he sat down under another one and he gazed back and it is said that he gazed unblinkingly for several days and nights!

What was he doing? He was opening a very long moment so that he could realise what actually is.

If you keep opening the moment and closing it, it's like a Groundhog day you only ever see the first, the same 10 seconds.So the key to realisation is to open up a moment and become absorbed, to sit in an unbroken moment that gets longer and longer and then you'll start seeing the truth about who or what you actually are.

Then you'll see how that connects with what else is and your realisation will come. Not from a book because it can't, only understanding can come from a book, but realisation coming from your direct experience of what is and that is gained by simply sitting in an opened moment.

When the Buddha opened his moment for several days and nights it was during this period that he realised profound truths about life which became the basis of his teaching.The whole truth is self evident when we know how to look.

The Distinction between Awareness and Consciousness

People often confuse the two and it's important to get it clear so here are some distinctions between awareness and consciousness. Let's look at Awareness first some of the names that awareness has are suchness beingness, isness and pure consciousness.

Some of the qualities that it has are that it's ungraspable, you're not going to grasp it and look at it.It's unreifiable you can't make it into something it's not a thing.It's described as sky-like ,it doesn't evolve, awareness doesn't change, awareness doesn't move, awareness underlies everything, awareness is the supreme intelligence, inconceivable In it's magnitude.

Awareness informs everything that appears and pervades everything that appears.Awareness never comes into being or goes out of being, awareness is not in one place more than another, awareness has no season,awareness isn't in one thing more than another,awareness isn't in one time more than another, before all time there was awareness, throughout all time there is awareness, after all creation is dissolved there is awareness remaining. Awareness is the domain in which all life in every way comes into being.

Now consciousness, is different and distinct, consciousness is the quality of something, there has to be an 'I' that has consciousness. Consciousness comes and goes, when we're in deep sleep, dreamless sleep, there is no consciousness, there's awareness but there's not consciousness. Why because consciousness needs an 'I'.

In deep sleep it is a fact that if you take someone's hand gently and put it in a bucket of warm water they will urinate! Why because they're aware, there's awareness of something happening which triggers an automatic response but it's not conscious. If you were conscious, if there was consciousness you wouldn't urinate.

Awareness never goes anywhere but consciousness does. There aren't states of awareness, there is just awareness but there are states of consciousness.

Consciousness has different kinds of qualities to it awareness has no qualities.Consciousness, we could say, is a function of awareness as everything else is as well.

In this relative conventional world where we find ourselve's there's this sense of 'I' that arises. Originally when we're born we don't have that sense of 'I' but as we get older and develop we start to interact and have the sense that there's somebody other than'I' ,there's the others and then that brings about thoughts and thoughts about identity develop and gradually we generate a separate platform of the 'I' that has its consciousness and then we start directing that consciousness which goes where we place our attention, into all the different things in the world. So that we might know what is and who I am and what life is.

After a while we realise that we're miserable that something inside is not fulfilled. Then finally we get to the point where (not finally hopefully before the end!) we get to the point where we place our consciousness onto awareness.We lift up our consciousness to awareness.

We find awareness and the result of that is it recognise's itself as bliss and the'I' is seen as a temporary phenomena which never had substantial existence, was always changing and had no defined boundary which means it was not real.

This is the hard thing to grasp just like a character in

my dream, when I was experiencing the character in my sleep dream that character certainly seemed to have substantial existence but when I woke up and recognised I was dreaming and that dreaming was just arising in my consciousness, I wasn't even the dreamer, I was the witness of the dreaming, and when I woke up to that truth I realised that none of it had any substantial existence what so ever and that even the consciousness states that I displayed in my dream were not real either they had no substantial existence, they only appeared to be real.

Perhaps I'm deeply asleep and I'm dreaming of meditating or I'm dreaming of having a profound experience, dreaming of Buddhas and it appears as a high state of consciousness in my dream but when I wake up I realise it had no substantial existence what's ever.No matter how it appeared the highest truth about it was that it was a dream.

What is real is that which allowed these states that I experience of waking, dreaming and sleeping to be.Truth is that which doesn't change-Awareness.

We couldn't say the sky was a thing couldn't we? You can't grasp it, you can't look at the sky, your senses can't detect the sky yet clearly the sky is there because that's where the clouds and the weather roll by. If there wasn't the sky where would they be? On this basis one might say the sky is like awareness and states of consciousness are what unfolds in that sky like awareness. Some days it's great billowing clouds - powerful states of consciousness and some days it's very fine and high serene, states of consciousness unfold in awareness as weather unfolds in the sky.

The weather is always changing just as there's no static state of consciousness, all states are continuously changing, transforming, moving but could we say that of the sky? Sky like awareness remains as transparent and unchanging as the sky.Does the sky have a centre? No consciousness sometimes appears to have a centre, awareness not.

Consciousness can be more in one place than another and sometime disappears altogether as in deep sleep. Awareness is the equally distributed substratum of all phenomena and circumstance.

When the psychological self is put down the part we're playing in this dream, the part we're playing in the movie of our life, when it's put down for a moment and we turn and look backwards to inquire what is looking out what we find is sky-like awareness. It's as if a human being is given the illusion of consciousness so that eventually it looks back and recognises that actually I'm a portal through which awareness experiences.

Awareness gives consciousness to a dream being (me) so that it might know itself, so that there might be a subject and an object, so that gratitude, wonder and joy might arise.

What you see is given by who you're being that it is.We think there's a fixed way about everything but there really isn't, who your being that it is gives you how you get it.When you completely stop being any way that it is and just let it be what it is without any projections upon it then consciousness and awareness align and then that's who I am.

Consciousness is the gift of awareness, consciousness is the great gift of this life, but what is the best thing to do with that consciousness?

Pour into my thinking? Waste it on trying to make something happen in this dream world or seek its source? The source of consciousness is awareness. We could say that consciousness is the dynamic aspect of awareness.

What would I see if I woke up here in this domain of wakefulness? First of all is there the possibility of a further awakening? I was a sleep dreaming then I woke up is there a possibility of awakening on this level is there perhaps a fourth state?

What is the awakening on this level what would I see if I awoke? Would I actually see that none of this has any inherent substantial reality that it's all dream like and what is real and unchanging is awareness, the truth, the absolute truth? The absolute truth and complete awakeness are the same.

We might say consciousness is how awareness looks into the dream, consciousness is the currency between beings in a dream and that all happens in unchanging awareness.This distinction of awareness and consciousness that opens up a new possibility of being of seeing because it's there all the time it's just been missed our consciousness has been going in the wrong direction.

Then at some point the consciousness returns and focuses and merges with awareness and there is the great revelation of what is real and what isn't real of what true joy is of what freedom really is, what the Self really is.

This brings the end of suffering because suffering only comes because we are ignorant of what the truth of it all is. Like when you're in a nightmare, you're thinking that that's really real, the dog with three heads is chasing you drooling and barking, chasing you towards a cliff and you'rein complete panic because you think that the whole thing is real but that isn't how it is then you wake up and realise that you were suffering because you forgot what is real what is unchanging, what is ever present, what is omniscient, what is omnipotent, what is inconceivable what is the source of all glory.

I forgot and my consciousness went elsewhere and I suffered. Then we can bring our consciousness back to the self awareness. That's a choice we can make.

What is Knowledge Reality?

"The Self which is knowledge is alone the reality. Knowledge of diversity is but false knowledge, This false knowledge which is but ignorance does not exist apart from the Self which is knowledge reality."
Ramana Maharshi

Let's have a look at this statement because our tendency can be to seek knowledge with a small k to seek information with our intellects.I remember hearing this story once about this guy and he's searching, searching for truth and he comes upon a temple and inside there are people all sitting thinking very deeply and he thinks 'ah this must be where people discover the truth, where they work the truth out through deep thinking and with highly honed intellects they eventually get to the truth'.

So he's sitting there and time goes by and eventually this little boy comes and pulls on his shirt and says 'come, come, come' and the guy goes 'no, don't disturb me, can't you see I'm thinking?'

The kid goes off and comes back again saying 'no come on, come on, come on' and then the guy goes 'okay what?'and the little kid was all shining and sparkly-eyed takes him out of the Temple of Reason and leads him on up the path and they come round the corner and there in front is this most fabulous city of crystal light and the very atmosphere is singing joyfully and the palaces are pulsating with the most beautiful vibration of love and his mind has become quiet and he's just looking and feeling intense awe and wonder.The little boy smiles happily.

It seems to us that the intellect is the vehicle to get to the Self or Knowledge but the intellect can only deal with knowledge in the realm of duality, the knowledge of things. In recent times and even literally in recent days the Chinese have developed and so have Google, a quantum computer that can do in three minutes what a supercomputer would take two billion years to do!

We've got enormous computing power now absolutely beyond what any one individual can really comprehend. With the advances made in ai which is now teaching itself through Deep Learning, we've taken the intelligence and the intellect to the absolute nth degree but is that bringing us Knowledge? It's not, it's processing data that generates information that gets assessed to give us knowledge with a small k. Does that really make any difference?

In the world of conventional reality it makes a difference but knowing that kind of knowledge doesn't really make a difference to the way that I am or my access to what is. We may know everything but we are surely none the wiser.

Self-knowledge is being the Self. Knowledge in the ultimate sense is beyond the intellectual level, the mind has to be focused rather than entertaining high thoughts. The intellect cannot reach the Self, it can talk about it,imagine it but it cannot reach it.

Knowledge, pure knowingness is actually everywhere all the time. By bringing one's consciousness to Knowledge with a capital K one awakens in a field of knowing where how it is is the greatest knowledge there is. Where being the self and relinquishing all lesser identities of being a body and I am what I do, I am what I think, I am the information that I have amassed, I am what I understand, relinquishing all of that and what remains is the unified field of knowingness where the truth is self-evident.

Wisdom is a name given to a certain kind of talking or the expression of certain kind of star spangled ideas. But the real wisdom is not made of ideas, the real wisdom is not made of thought, the real wisdom is the Self, pure undifferentiated knowingness.

True Knowing is not about what comes from processing data and turning it into information and then getting knowledge but Knowledge in its ultimate sense comes from direct experience. It's not about believing something or about deducing through the use of logic whether something should exist or not. The real knowing is when you directly experience what is. There is the possibility of direct knowing, direct experience where each individual realises the Self, the truth, this is really possible in a human life.

Techniques and practises are empty things. What is fullness? People talk about being fulfilled as if fulfilment comes from a set of circumstances. I had these set of circumstances and I became fulfilled, I got what I wanted then I was fulfilled but that kind of fulfilment comes and goes it's here today gone tomorrow.

What is the real fulfilment? The real fulfilment is the Self that fills emptiness and each time we open up to that, the fulfilment just wells up and there it is for no reason other than that's what is.

'Be still and Know that I am God' that is a statement from the Bible. It does not say to know God read the Bible a lot and it does not say listen to the priests and pray all the time, be a good person, no that's not what is said. If you want to know God the instruction is simple- be still. Still body, still mind and when we calm right down all that is the Self and that's true Knowledge, there's a sense of completeness and each time we come into that place that's home that's where the thirst is quenched, the thirst to know. when we become still we align with what is everywhere all the time the substratum of all life-God. Only by being the Self does wisdom in its ultimate sense arise. Can we see this?

If an individual wants to become wise at the moment what the individual will do is read books, listen to teachings but what those teachings are really saying is if you want to become wise immerse yourself in the field of Wisdom. Understanding is not wisdom.

Take the filters off, the filters of your preferences, the filters of your conditionings and opinions take them off and surface and unfold in what actually is always, already here, the luminous, transparency, the substratum of every moment.

The presence of knowingness is in all things, in all states, unmoving and unchanging. This is wisdom. By immersing ourselves in that field of pure knowing that's how we become wise and harmoniously connected to what essentially is.

The Distinction Between the Heart and the Mind

Different traditions have different understandings about the heart and the mind so as I use these terms I want to be clear about what how it is for me. Christianity for example: I said to my niece she should follow her heart she said oh no and she quoted something from the Bible' The heart is deceitful above all things, and it is desperately sick: who can know it? In Buddhism they have different definitions for it but what I mean is this.

In truth there isn't actually a distinction it's all one but for the sake of understanding it's good to make this distinction because when you distinguish between two things you open up a new space, a new possibility of being. Something new can come out of that distinction.

The mind is where mental states happen, mental states are everything to do with thinking, remembering, memory and the creation of possibility. Moods and emotions and states of consciousness also happen in the Mind. The mind is the home of internal dialogue, chatter and commentary.

In the heart there is no thinking. The heart doesn't think the heart is the domain of silence, the heart is a domain of pure knowing, the heart is the domain of wisdom.

When I sleep my consciousness, which all day has been looking at mental states returns into my heart and I lose all consciousness of mental states and all consciousness of 'I' but I'm not dead am I? If if a mosquito landed on my face I'd probably just automatically swat it off, if a draft came I'd probably just automatically turn over without having to go through the conscious self or if someone put my hand in warm water when I was in deep dreamless sleep I would actually urinate! Because there was awareness there. All the time there's awareness in every part of the body but not consciousness. In sleep the consciousness returns into the heart, the heart is where I am and who I am sitting in the heart the source point of my witnessing that isn't broken that isn't damaged that isn't influenced by anything that doesn't evolve that doesn't change and who I am in the mental realm is an ongoing construct thoughts feed the mind.

The heart doesn't actually experience emotions the heart only has feelings, the heart is feeling and it's the mind that experiences emotions. Emotions are always about coming from the past and they're always triggered by thought.

You're watching a movie and something happens and you have a thought about it you recognise it and it triggers an emotion that you've been carrying. That has not been fully resolved so it comes up again triggered by something different this time, but it comes up again and it keeps on coming till it's resolved.

Emotions don't come from the world they come from me, they come from my pain body. For example two people witness one person die and they have two different reactions to the death of that person. One person who is very attached to the dying person experiences tremendous grief and another person who hated that person who died experienced a feeling of gladness 'I'm glad they've gone I never liked them".

Clearly the person dying did not emanate an experience otherwise they both would have got it the same way.The experience of dying or anything else doesn't emanate an experience in itself otherwise we'd all get it that way.Who we're being that the dying is gives us the experience we get.

The emotions don't emanate from what triggered them. There emotions are to do with our unresolvedness and our ignorance of what truly is.

Emotions are there, they're not wrong they're just how it is until you resolve them and clear your emotional backlog which then allows you to come into presence and when you're present to the heart you'll find that there are no negative feelings in the heart. There are no negative feelings there is no sorrow, there there's no grief, there you are joy, you are freedom, peace, love. There you're not feeling love, you're not feeling peace but you actually are that there.

In the world of the heart there's no sorrow, there's no anger there's none of that there's flowing as awareness and you are it, you're not experiencing it. Whereas when you're in the mind, in the mental states then these emotions do come, the emotions are there and that's what contributes to our suffering.

Some say 'I want to feel misery, anger and pain because it's who I am, it's what life is.Without suffering how would you know joy?'It is what life is until you go deeper and you can move beyond that. There is a joy that is self effulgent, it shines it's own glory and does not need pain to give it context.

As you start to flow and live in a heart-based reality you will notice that sorrow diminishes and what is there is true understanding.

Even when somebody dies, there's grief, the passing of things causes so much grief in people, the passing of what's going on now. Grief and anxiety, these are emotions but where did these emotions spring from do they actually come out of the events or is it what we make of the events that causes the emotions?

We are the generator of the emotions and the emotions are all about what we haven't realised from the past and what we've made of the past and the meanings that we've given the past. So then events happen in the present and triggers those old meanings and so what has not been fully felt comes up and there it is again. If we really saw life as it truly is there is no cause for grief or sorrow, the passing of an old friend would not be a cause for sorrow.

Seeing from the heart-based reality, knowing how life actually is of course we have preferences, we rather they were here than gone but even those preferences are coming out of mental states, coming out of the mind and there's a place of equanimity, there's a place of joy, there's a place of seeing how life is and there it's not like you don't care for others but you've realised that the personality and the psychological self that you were identifying as that experienced all the emotions to give it some sense of self actually you don't need to do that and you're not that so what you find is you become a channel through which love flows as compassion.

You can't act compassion, when we're in a heart-based reality when we're not there as chundering psychological selves, then compassion can flow through us unobstructed. So much of the time we are giving but we're giving with an agenda which means that it's not really true generosity.

In the heart based reality there's no agendas, the giving is giving, the kindness is really kindness the generosity is really generous without any hidden agendas.

This is a wonderful place to come from because it's so simple and the feelings are real and oceanic in their depth because when you're living in the mind and you also got the world of emotions as part of a mentally based reality, you never know when they're going to come up because anything can trigger them. Your unfelt sadness about anything can be triggered by a movie, can be triggered by something somebody said or by a piece of music anything can trigger it. We don't really want to feel our pain so we suppress it, sit on it which has the effect of limiting out capacity to feel so increasingly we live into a thought based reality which we think is under our control. We don't notice that this mentally based reality experience has no joy in it or love or peace.

We feel happy because we have just bought something we wanted or we are unhappy because we couldn't get what we wanted. This is contrived and conditional happiness and not the happiness we felt as a child. We can live like that and without really noticing it our range of experience diminishes until basically we become just a set of habits with no spontaneity, growth over fun.

The other possibility is going behind that, recognizing that whatever I experience I only know I'm experiencing it because I'm witnessing it. Rather than looking at what I'm experiencing: my thoughts, my mental states, my emotions to see what's behind that what does it feel like to witness those things?

What does it feel like when I step out of the part that I'm playing? Take all the masks off, who is there?

The mental states are an attribute of the part I'm playing,the thoughts are an attribute of the part I'm playing, the dramas that happen are an attribute of the part that I'm playing. What happens when I step behind that, go off stage for a moment, go off the set for a moment?

The heart is amazing because it is the source of your

breath and the divine principle that motivates it and the source of the sense 'I am' from which thoughts come is traced back to the heart also. The witness is the heart awareness which looks through the individual heart into the creation and all its wonders.

The amazing thing is that although there's this sense 'I am my heart' this heart is also connected to all life and everything is seen as heart from this place. So there's a strange kind of paradox on the one hand you are an individual heart but when one is in there one senses unity and totality of the heart with all life.

Our pain comes because we are thinking that we're the thinker. We are thinking that our thoughts are a reflection of how life actually is and we don't get that our thoughts are actually a product of our mood or who we're being in that moment of thinking. Over time this misunderstanding creates a completely false sense of self and life. We believe we are the thinker and accept everything that it delivers.

Who you are being that life is gives you how you get it, life does not emanate anything. If we can understand that a major break through happens. Life doesn't emanate anything if life emanated something to us we would all get it but we don't we all get everything differently and we actually get everything differently each time we encounter it.

This is very unnerving so we try and solidify things and come to some sort of consensus, this is this and that is that but it isn't that how we get it is given by who we're being that it is. And that's the strain and stress of living in the mind, living as the thinker, identifying as the part we play.

Thinking that our thoughts are born of reality when in fact they're just born of a mood or whatever happened just prior to that thought arising.

But behind that this peace. behind that is the observer, behind that there's the witness and the witness is the portal into awareness. The witness is like the lens and what's looking out through that lens is a witness awareness.

The heart is where silence is, the heart is where peace is and the mind is noise and chatter. All the time trying to develop different mental states or change and manipulate mental states in order to get something that we think will bring satisfaction. But it never really works because everything is so fleeting but there is something that you don't have to manipulate anything to get because you already are it and that's the heart when you're flowing as the heart there's no mistakes everything is appropriate.

It gets easy to be there again and again and recognise that in some incredible way you don't ever actually leave it.

When you're flowing as the heart you can completely disappear and still be enjoying immensely this life unfolding because how we get this life is a reflection of where we're looking from if we're looking from the mind we could be in paradise and still not really be able to connect and enjoy because we're dominated by a mood generated out of our thoughts. If we're flowing as a heart then you can see heaven you're not obstructing yourself, you're not interfering, you're not in your own way, you've gone quiet and you're complete and you're aware you can see what actually is, how extraordinary and wonderful and amazing it actually is!

The heart knows, the heart is the seat of knowledge we have to bring our attention out of the world, out of mental states, out of our thinking, out of our emotions, out of our dramas and bring it back into the heart, it is what happens every night when we sleep. To do that without being asleep is what they call Samadhi, the samadhi of the natural state which is unsurpassed.

It is not even a state it's just how it is and I am and it's here in the heart that this subject /object paradigm collapses and I am what I'm feeling and what I'm feeling is really indescribable and not supported by inner or outer senses.

When you bring the consciousness to awareness there's bliss but there is no one measuring it or talking about it. In the mental world there's always measurements going on 'oh I'm quite happy today, I'm not exactly where I was yesterday. I was really happy back then!' all the time measuring 'oh I don't like this I do like that I don't like that person. That's true, that's not true, that's quite true'. All the time measuring but in the heart there's none of that there's just this beautiful flowing feeling being what is and that's literally heaven.

Heaven on earth and that's freedom, that's liberation. Liberation from thinking I'm the thinker. Liberation from identifying as the mind and all its nonsense, liberation from the suffering that comes from being run by emotions and the necessity to avoid them or the addiction to them.

The heart that I'm talking about cannot break. The true heart never gets broken, the true heart is the ultimate refuge and it turns out I am that heart.

Being the heart then the breath, the energy of life is love. Being in the mind love is more like a transaction or a negotiated agreement, an expectation or a fabrication.

Emotions vs Feelings

What is the difference between emotions and feelings? Many people confuse the two, they think they are the same they think that emotions and feelings are the same and they're really not.

If you accept this distinction between your emotions and your feelings then by creating that distinction a new space, a new possibility of being comes into play.

Emotions, everybody knows the saying 'you're never angry about what you're angry about' you're also never sad about what you're sad about. Emotions always are triggered by thoughts, something happens, your mind interprets it and the interpretation then demands you feel an emotion.

You see the puppy dog fall into a puddle and then your mind says 'oh that is so sad the puppy dog fell in the puddle' so then it tells you what is the appropriate emotion to run from your stock of unresolved emotions, through your body/mind mechanism.

However by this time you're out of the now, it wasn't a spontaneous feeling, even though the emotion sometimes feels spontaneous if you actually look it goes: recognition of what's happening, find corresponding emotion, run the emotion through your body.

The emotions are stored in your pain body and you carry them with you until they are resolved. We keep getting them triggered until they are fully felt and resolved. When you feel sadness or grief it's always the same sadness, it's always the same grief, no matter what the circumstance that triggered it that time was.

With feelings it's different. Feelings are not there because of anything, emotions are there because of something. Your mind interprets life and because of that you have an emotion. The emotions we carry come from the past situations that happened that we didn't fully integrate the experience of at the time.

Emotions are when your mind encapsulates feelings and labels them and gives them meaning. We generate meanings about the dramas that we've lived and we support those meanings with emotions. It's an entirely fabricated thing.

Feelings on the other hand are different, when your emotional body is cleared even if it's just for a moment, then the feeling of life, the present, the Presence emerges. It's a bit like when the movie is stopped being projected onto the screen there's just this incredible blank but that blank isn't null and void, there is a feeling, these feelings we give them names like unconditional love, joy, gratitude, peace, clarity and freedom.

There are no negative feelings in the universe, there's no sorrow inherently existing in the universe. There's no anger inherently existing in the universe. When we become free we do not experience anger or sorrow, those are emotions and they come from misunderstanding how life is. Angels don't get angry, angels you don't get sad, there's no fighting going on in Heaven!

Why because there is no actual inherently existing cause of anger or any wholly existing cause of sorrow for one who sees what is clearly.

The fact that something dies is not sad, the fact that somebody dies is not sad otherwise we'd all get it as sad but we don't. Some people think 'thank God he's gone" some people think 'oh my god it is so sad, he's gone' dependent on who their being that that person was to them. Their grief is given by their meanings that they have invented. The emotion of grief does not emanate from the dead person.

This is an incredible thing because we tend to look at grief or sorrow, anger, jealousy, all the different emotions that run through us, we tend to look at them as real, we give them reverence but they actually just need to be felt, they keep on returning until we do feel them. Until we do acknowledge, accept, and recognise that actually they come from somewhere way back then and are just waiting for resolution. As we clear 'the there then' we fully arrive in 'the here now'

In the same way that with physical pain if it reaches a certain threshold we pass out, if say as a child we experience highly impactful experiences then the emotional reaction is deferred until such time as we can absorb it which we might do over years a bit at a time.

It's possible to clear the backlog of unresolved emotion to clear the pain body. It's possible to clear the backlog of unresolved anger to actually get to the core and the root of the anger, the root of the sadness and to resolve it so that you move from being an emotional person to being a person who can feel massively without a fear of being overwhelmed.

When you experience emotions it's always the one feeling the emotion and the emotion itself. When you have feelings it's only one thing that is going on, the feeling is happening, it's a living thing, it's not me feeling it, it's just the event of a clear space, a self cognising wonder, the feeling of life happening.

Whereas in emotions it's me feeling the emotion, me calling the emotion up.

It's an amazing break through when you get this that if you're feeling an emotion that the meaning of it comes from somewhere outside of that moment. This moment that you feel the emotion in has just triggered it for re-examination, for integration and resolution. Causeless joy and happiness become stable as we clear the emotional body.

The feeling of happiness is the feeling of life and is not derived from circumstances going well but just the experience of life itself you don't really know that you're happy because you're not there measuring it and there's no commentary about it. When you feel deep peace you don't really know the depth of that peace because there's nobody there measuring it or commentating about it .

We become increasingly stable in clarity and happiness as the emotional body empties itself and becomes resolved.

Emotions are always called forth by thought, feelings naturally arise out of presence. Emotions are conditioned responses, feelings spontaneously appear from the heart of life.

Emotions keep returning until resolution comes, feelings of peace underscore all phenomena. Emotions are triggered by the interpretation of events, feelings flow free from thought. Emotions are generated in the body/mind and feelings soar in awareness. Emotions appear in time and drama, feelings are only ever in the now. Emotions are projected so they can be seen, feelings emerge from nothing as all there's ever been.

As we awaken, we are heading away from the turbulence of emotions into the deep world of pure feeling where the egoic self that suffers, dissolves into an ocean of feeling. The Self is seen as pure feeling, the seer, the seeing and what is seen are then one. The feeling, the feeler and what is felt are the same.

The Natural State

What is the natural state?

It's not really a state it's more like the sub stratum, the basis, the infinite basis upon which finite states are projected, upon which thoughts appear, upon which everything happens. The natural state is what is always already present, the ground of being and when we disentangle ourselves from relative, temporary states and perceptions, immediately again we become aware of suchness, the natural state. It never changes,it's completely alive. It's not static but it never changes It's endlessly peaceful, there's no depth to the peace that it is, it's complete silence that is underneath whatever noise there might be. Because of the natural state we can safely vanish meaning that we can let go of identifying as the part we play in life, we can let go of being male or female, let go of coming from a certain place, let go of identifying with the past.

Let go of everything that changes, let go of all identity whatever you think you are that isn't who you are.

Many think' I am what I've done all the things that I've done, the sum total of all of that and what I've made of all of that, that is definitely who I am"- no it's not! You're much more amazing than that but the interrogator, the commentator, the characteriser the know it all, it can't come in, we have to put that down then what really is, what doesn't come and go becomes apparent and obvious.

If we spend a little time surrendered to the natural state, a sensation in the heart starts to develop and it's as if we get pulled out of the mind, pulled out of the head and pulled into the heart and this life seen from the perspective of the heart is seen as a heaven!

When your mind is quiet you can see, how perfect every minute detail of creation actually is. It's not like somebody has seen all of it just like it's not like anybody knows everything, the natural state is omniscience, it's pure knowingness without limit or crystallisation.

By putting down what we thought we were, but are actually not, we can allow space for what truly is.The gravity of the heart is felt more and more by remaining as the natural state, the most extraordinary miracle occurs which is it's seen that the natural state is love. Unconditional all pervading love, we then realise for ourselves that the substratum of life, all life, is love. This is what the heart knows and this is what prevails when we let the natural state be.

It comes when it will but once really seen that's enough you don't forget it, it's not a state that is developed by practice it's a profound or perhaps the most profound insight that you get in a moment in time that stays with you forever, you're able to distinguish suchness from everything else, you're able to distinguish presence from everything else.

Following that you realise that this suchness and this presence actually pervades everything and is what reality is and these temporary forms of planets spinning, forests, trees, mountains. people and all the endless things we create these are all temporary and not actually substantial or real, they're all figments of a dream. The natural state is pure awakeness.

If you are completely awake what would your life perception be? and would it still be you looking at something? No!

The more time we allow, surrender and submit to the natural state on the deepest of levels we feel secure to let go of what we've been hanging on to that causes us problems but gives us a sense of identity. And the more functional you become mentally, you let go of baggage that you don't need to be bringing with you everywhere, you don't need to have to maintain an identity, you don't need to have to defend an identity or an attack for an identity. Why? Because you found something much more wonderful.

In the natural state nothing's measured, nothing's remembered and nothing's forgotten, no thought is more important than any other.

To be able to vanish and let things be that's what it is to be free.

Where does the 'I" originate?

The sense that I am, the sense that I am separate, the sense that I am unique, the sense that I am a being, where does it originate and is it actually the truth?

It's a very convincing feeling. In the Buddhist view of course one of the main things about the Buddhist view is that it's saying 'no self' there isn't actually a self there. What it means by that is that there isn't a substantially existing, separate self, there isn't an independent entity that is self-sustained that is self-perpetuating.

If we look at the Self there is a strong sense of self and there is a dynamic of the self but it's not independent and it's not substantial and it's not real, it's as real as everything else that exists in the dream.

So this sense of I where does it originate?

Getting to the origin of 'I' the first thing we have to be clear about is that we're not talking about the 'I' as in who your name represents, the part you play in this life, the ego identity, we're not talking about your body we're not talking about the 'I' that has momentum through space and time, having experience and working it out and processing and so forth we're not talking about that 'I' we're talking about the essential 'I'. The divine principle manifest at the core, that causes breath to come from which our thoughts arise, the observer, the 'I AM'.

The great yogi Ramana Maharshi discovered an incredibly simple way to come to the answer because we don't want another set of ideas because they're confusing and they don't bring us to the reality of what is anyway, his suggestion was, his clue was to find the source of your breath. The breath is something that gives you a tremendous sense of individuality doesn't it the breath unites our body, the vehicle, with consciousness and keeps us in space and time. Without the breath we disappear into timelessness, we lose our individual sense of self and the dream disappears.

So the breath is the source of our sense of being a separate self, no one breathes your breath and your breath is the dynamic that keeps you all together, keeps all the different levels of being together.

Also what makes us fairly convinced that we are separate individuals is our thoughts, no one has your thoughts and so what Maharshi is saying is that if you follow your thoughts back to where they actually arise from, this sense of I, you will have a revelation about the true nature of I .If you follow your breath back which also gives you the sense of being separate and individual you will also have the same realisation. So the breath and the thinking arise from the same place and they are the causes our of our sense of having a self.

He mentioned a technique which is incredibly simple but actually works really well, when we're trying to find the origin of the 'I'.

The technique was simply just to go 'I-I-I-I' and take your consciousness to what is happening take your attention to what is happening within energetically as you simply say that. If you keep going with it without any expectation or without bombing it with thought and you just keep going 'I-I-I-I' you'll start to find that it vibrates in the heart that it all comes from the heart and when we come to that place we come out of the mental realm where the 'I' was the ego, we come out of the psychological self and we enter into pure being and behold the divine principle of life that breathes us.

We enter into the realm of the witness, we go beyond the intellect and the witness is the source of 'I' and is the source of our point of view, our unique point of view.

When we come into the witness what we realise

there, amazingly, is that there is an interface between awareness and consciousness. There has to be an 'I' around which is consciousness and when we bring that consciousness which is a temporary phenomena of the 'I',when we bring that to itself and then to awareness, we realise that the truth about us is that the 'I' sense originates out of awareness and it's a function of awareness in the form of consciousness.

It temporarily creates a platform where we can objectify ans look at things and where we can be a subject of what is happening.But the truth is that what is unchanging is the awareness and there isn't actually an 'I' there, there isn't actually anyone sitting there, it's just a temporary sense of 'I' an illusion.

Keep doing it and after a while you'll start to feel something and if you do it for a long time you'll feel a lot it's a very powerful technique hiding behind a very simple form but it's actually very, very powerful in terms of bringing you back here to the point that you witness from, to the point that your breath arises from,to the point that your thought arises from.

If you keep doing it there's a kind of burning that starts to happen and you start to move back into the heart. We have poured our consciousness out into the world and out into the many levels of our mind and this technique, and others, draw you back so that you can bring all of you back just as you would do if you were in sleep. In a deep dreamless sleep there's no consciousness, in a deep dreamless sleep it's all been brought back into the cave of the heart and the trick is to be able to do this while being awake, to bring all of you back, all right back to the seed'I' in the heart.

The level of experience beyond thought shows you the truth about what the 'I' is and its relationship to unchanging awareness and the distinction between consciousness and awareness, consciousness has to have an 'I' that is conscious but in awareness there is no 'I'.

Awareness is like the massive river the Ganga flowing and the'I' is like a ripple or a swirl in it. To have this work you need to be able to let go of your current sense of what 'I' means because as long as you're identifying as who you think you are they'll be suffering and you will not be able be the 'I' beyond thought.

Anytime that your mind is too loud just do this exercise. When you're not doing anything during the day, when you're walking about, when you're doing housework, when you're going from a to b, when you're in the supermarket, when you're driving, this is an exercise you can do. It has very beneficial effects, even doing a little, a few moments and the experience comes of what is prior to thinking, what is before the persona, the source of this sense 'I'.

The 'am' that the 'I' originates from is life, awareness itself. The simple sense 'I am' where all of your consciousness and all of your experience actually originates from.

The 'I' is like the pure drop and the awareness is the ocean and that drop can dissolve ultimately, hopefully while you're alive, into the ocean. Actually we can let go of the sense 'I' all together but first to find it, first to come to that heart cave. When we come to that cave it becomes much easier to let the breath slow right down and perhaps stop for longer and longer periods and in these timeless moments the truth of awareness unfolds. What actually is, at that point not even an experience because that implies an experiencer. The experience and the person having it but when we come to that deep place there is just what is, life itself it's self cognising. Meaning that it's not a subject looking at an object, we've gone beyond that and there just is what is, pure life, pure intelligence, inconceivable wonder that generates, operates and destroys all that is, yet remains completely unchanged, and we are that.

The ignorant and the Wise

To the ignorant the world is the sole existent reality, to the wise that formless infinite being which underlies the world is the one reality. Ramana Maharshi

Raman Maharshi was a a great master that lived at the foot of Arunachala mountain in Tamil Nadu, India. Some people say that although he's gone now, he's the most alive of all dead gurus, his spirit and his teaching is very present and very vibrant. He had made some really amazing statements and here's one.

When we sleep dream it's a very vivid dream there are people in it there's forms in it, there's space in it, there's the appearance of time in it, there's the appearance of consciousness. The characters that I'm interacting with in my dream appear to have consciousness, they're talking to me I'm talking to them we're feeling but when I wake up I realise that what appeared so real in my dream had no substantial reality whatsoever. It wouldn't be true to say that it didn't exist at all because I was experiencing it so in some lesser sense it did exist but it didn't have substantial reality. The car that I was driving in was not actually real the people that I was talking to they were not actually real. The consciousness that I thought they had, they didn't actually have it because they didn't actually exist.

Everybody has that experience when they sleep dream and wake up they go 'oh it was a dream' and sometimes in the dream you get the possibility of waking up actually while you're still dreaming and that's lucid dreaming then you can direct the dream to go the way you want it to go. Generally speaking as soon as you realise you're dreaming you wake up.

What is it that that dream was actually made of? The forms that appeared they were empty of anything substantial, they were just dreamt up but they appeared and they were made of a substance, the substance of dream. It's easy to see when you look at a sleep dream that every part of that dream is made of the same thing just like a movie.

When you're watching it, it seems very real and it seems to have substantial reality, it seems to be affecting you but then the truth of it is that it's all made of the same thing it's all light projected through two-dimensional film to give the impression of substantial existence but of course it doesn't have that existence it is projected onto a screen.

Here he's saying to the wise that the formless infinite being which underlies the world is the one reality. He's saying that just as in a sleep dream everything is made of the same substance and that the underlying reality of a dream is the fact that there is a dreamer. The dream is not chosen by anything it arises of its own accord given by the causes and conditions that preceded it. So the dream consciousness under lied all the content of the dream.

In this reality where we find ourselves now can we recognize what is already always present everywhere equally?

Again using that brilliant example of the sky, the sky is formless is n't it you couldn't say the sky had a form in order to be have a form you would need edges to define it. There's no edge to the sky, there's no qualities there's nothing graspable about the sky yet strangely it must be there for the weather to have a place to be in, for the stars and the galaxies to have a place to exist, for space to have a home.

The sky underlies every kind of weather condition that happens. For us can we see what is present in every conscious moment it doesn't matter what you're being conscious of but in every moment that we're awake there's something identical to any other moment that we were in, it underlies the drama of our life. So the weather is the dramas that unfold for us, the thoughts that we think, the feelings that we have and the states of consciousness that we have. These are all aspects of the weather that happens in this all-pervading sky-like awareness. Freedom is recognizing that on the level of experience it's not a long climb up a steep mountain you've already done that now it's just a simple seeing.

The part we play in the movie is what we do, the form we take,the thoughts that we think, the expressions that we project and the states of consciousness that we inhabit. All of that is the part we're playing in the movie of life. But by virtue of what is all that happening? What is the underlying, the formless infinite being?

Awareness is not an object you can't objectify it you can't make it into a thing it's not a thing like the sky isn't a thing.

You might say this world is real, 'look I can pinch myself and I will feel pain, that's a real body and that's real pain.' You might say this substantially exists but it doesn't substantially exist. For a thing to be real which nothing is, there are certain things that have to be present. For example (there may be more significators than I'm going to list). It needs to be born of something real, obviously what is real cannot be born of what is unreal. If you dream a sleep dream of going to a car manufacturing plant and you dream that you make a car in your sleep dream it won't actually be there as real in this reality when you wake up because something real can't be born of something unreal. The second one if it's real it has to be completely independent, not relying on anything else to support it in any way. Also it cannot have any constituent parts. if it had constituent parts then the name we give a car is a designation to a whole load of different elements but there isn't actually one thing that is the car.

We couldn't say the engine was the engine because it's made up of so many constituent parts, we couldn't say those constituent parts were substantially existing either because they're made up of an infinity of atomic particles, so not substantially existing .

Another thing for it to be real is it would have to have an edge a clearly defined edge that separated it from everything else. But nothing does because as soon as we turn the microscope on, what we see is what appears like an edge of my computer or the edge of my hand actually is a blur of subatomic particles there is no edge, I flow into the environment there is no point where I begin and it ends.

Another significator of something being real must be that it does not evolve or change and is always the same and seen the same way by everyone as its not subject to interpretation or projection because it emanates an indisputable self.

Nothing in this world has those qualities everything is dependent on everything else everything is made up of constituent parts, nothing has an edge.It's all dreamlike.

What Ramana Maharshi says here to the wise that formless infinite being which underlies the world is the one reality. That formless infinite being is it subject to time and change? Was it born of something? Does it have constituent parts? No on all counts. No, time unfolds in it but it is not governed by time.

Does it have a size or dimension? No space happens within it yet itself has no size or shape. All things that have size and shape happen within this infinite being, the formless infinite being which underlies all reality, these stratum, the screen on which the whole thing is projected, the sky in which all weather (phenomena) unfold.

By understanding this we can perhaps come into a place where we experience that by discounting everything that is not, if we discount everything that we know to be temporary and all things because reality is not a thing, you come into a beautiful place.

We discount the environment because it's filled with temporal things and we have a body but we know we're not our body we are within it.

Sometimes you might have an experience, maybe as a child or when you had an operation or when you nearly died, where you looked back and saw your body completely still and you were separate from it. So you're not the body but then even the thing that you were when you looked back on your body you actually perceived that as well.

This awareness that gives birth to consciousness and the sense of 'I'. That awareness is the underlying reality not the sense of 'I'. The sense of 'I' comes and goes. 'I am' was here before the 'I'. I is an event in consciousness that without without an 'I' there can't be consciousness only awareness. Awareness has no 'I' then 'I' comes and awareness gives birth to consciousness around an 'I' that perceive so that the universe can know itself, a temporary platform to look at the object of creation.

The answer to these questions is not in the mental realm the answer to this question is being able to distinguish the underlying substratum of all experience. To watch the movie but be present to the screen gives you the right relationship to the movie, to distinguish and be awareness whilst living out a story gives you the correct relationship to all that is.

The content or the story has no substantial existence and does not emanate from the events but from the minds that interpret them and that can be a bit shocking because we think it's real, we know dreams aren't real except when we're having them but we think this is real except when we wake up. This is what he's saying: to the ignorant, the world is the sole existent reality, what is going on here, the weather today, the ticking of the clock, the breath that just came in and just came out, what I'm going to do next, what I did just before that's the sole reality.

To the wise that formless infinite being which underlies the world is the one reality.

Death, dying and the Bardos

What happens when you die?

I had a near-death experience some years ago and that took the shape of me sitting with a friend and suddenly I started to feel a tremendous upsurge of energy like a wind within me, very powerfully, so I tried to breathe and hold that wind together and control it. But it's not happening it's like a massive rush heading upwards and it reached a point where I knew that I just had to let go, there was no other option. So I let go and then there was like a blank and the next thing I know is I'm looking up a tube and at the top it's the beautiful light sparkling and inviting. Calling me upwards to this beautiful white and blue light. I go up towards it quite slowly ascending up and then for some reason I just slowed down and stopped. I looked to the left and I looked all-around and I can see all that's ever happened or will ever happen or indeed could ever happen was all happening in unchanging awareness and then I said to myself "I am that".

At that point somebody behind me, who I didn't see but knew was my guardian angel from previous experiences, said "that is why you've been meditating all this time".

I thought it meant at the time that my meditation created this result but later I realised that actually the meditation, what it had done is that it had given me sufficient equanimity, sufficient calmness to be able to see exactly what is happening and who I am and what the truth is and not to be overrun by fear and panic. That is what happens once you come out of your body at the time of death or any other time it can be very frightening. You're in a completely different world and a lot happens very quickly. Now ideally you go straight on up through to the light. I came back by the way! Obviously, here I am!

You go straight on up to the light and all is well.However not everybody does that. Basically what distracts us at that important moment is momentums of fear or desire. If you have any kind of sense of specialness for example which you are clinging to or any other strong identity, in fact anything that is in your mind, when the energy arises massively as you come out of your body, at the time of death the energy can go into that fantasy of being special or what ever and inflate it.

Just like when someone who is not dead comes off medication, the release of energy that the medication had been suppressing pours into any fantasy that they had and the next thing they know they're wandering around thinking they're Queen Victoria. The same thing happens at the time of death.

There's one person I know who died and who had spent his whole life trying to propagate peace in the world just really was committed to it and he'd had quite a lot of success doing it to quite a large number of people. Sometime after his death he came to me in a dream and he's telling me very excitedly that he has figured out the way to bring world peace. It involves me talking to specific people. He had a bundle of what looked like initially scrolls that he'd written all the conversations that needed to be had with everybody in order for everybody to get the common sense of world peace and get on with the job of living and loving. But as he handed it to me it turned into rags and he was in a complete delusion about his own influence or power. Clearly he had spent a great amount of time and effort making these plans in some domain. When he was alive on earth he obviously thought this about himself but he was functional but when the energy released at death went up into this illusion it distracted him from his journey to the light.

There was another man who lived in a town where he was quite a bigwig and his idea of specialness was that he was superior to everybody else, better educated than everybody else and he had a secret sense that he could be a president or a real leader but it never really showed up in his actual life. At the time of death he did not go up into the light, the energy hit and inflated this fantasy of being special and he was seen walking through the Bardo's as a Hungry Ghost His hair was falling out as he dragged his wife, who he wouldn't let go of, full of puff and pride going nowhere, completely in a delusion that he was something that he wasn't. Very sad to see.

Also at the time of death people go into denial refusing to accept what has happened. I found another man who I knew well, in a bar, holding a beautiful glass of lager, golden and sparkling. His hair was disheveled and he was wearing his normal clothes but he was ghostly, another Hungry Ghost. I said to him what are you doing here? 'I am waiting for my chums' was his reply. I said 'even if they came they wouldn't be able to see you and you're not going to be able to drink that beautiful lager, you're not supposed to be here, you must go on.'

There was another situation where I had befriended a man who was an authentic yogi, who had lived in India for over 25 years. He was a great mystic and could traverse the different planes of existence at will.His name was Mira Baba and I met him in India and he came over to England and stayed with us for a year. During that time he would do things like go off into the astral worlds and find people who had died of heroin overdoses but hadn't realised they'd died and he would bring them into a great big toy rabbit that he had found in the street and he would shout at them, talk to them, ring bells, rattle his damaru (drum). He would do this for two or three days and nights non-stop and finally they realised that actually they were dead and needed to go on.

The adepts of his tradition do not like to be stalked by the Angel of Death so he chose to take his own life when he saw fit. Which he duly did ceremoniously. When he died, because I was close to him and had been serving him, I was able to see over the next three weeks or so his his progress through all the levels of transition. The first level was that after he left his body seven beings that look very like him with a beard, top knots, Rudra beads, etheric Shiva sadhus came and got him from the lower realms and lifted him up out of where he was.

Then he had a guru at the very beginning of his journey. In this lifetime he was initiated by his root guru and then I saw him come into the presence of his guru. He was sitting on a raised couch with several of his devotees sitting next to him in a very relaxed, happy atmosphere and in front of the

Guru was a big circular disc. Then Baba came streaming onto the disc.

He was full of pride and pomp and all puffed up with ego. He came in and stood in front of the Guru on this disc about seven and a half feet tall, full of it. The Guru gently with his foot tapped the toe of Baba and then Baba started to shrink. He shrunk till he was about the size of a cockroach and everybody laughed not at Baba but at the stupidity of the ego. The energies that we gather as an ego in a dream we do not take with us. Then the next scene that happened was that he progressed into this kind of zone or chamber where all the energies of his life were brought together as huge sphere, the only energies that remained that he could have that were him and his were the energies gathered whilst he was in presence. When he wasn't in his mind, when he was just a character in a play, none of that came with him or had any real relevance any more. But every moment that he gathered light as presence was his and it got condensed and purified and condensed. The sphere started quite big and was condensed and condensed and condensed and till it was about the size of a baseball, very potent and shining.

Then he was asked what form did he want and he said' I want to keep my my Baba form 'he had a name for his form which was with a turban and sitting on a carpet with his special mystical equipment that he would fly around the place on. So then the light ball was given back to him and it disappeared into his form then he shot off. The last I saw of him he was out in some very, high faraway heaven, where there was virtually no time at all, there was a great light there and he sat absorbed for who knows how long.

In our lives much of our desire energy is focused into sex and throughout our lives we generate enormous amounts of desire which we use to become aroused in our pursuit of orgasmic pleasure.I had a dream it's one of the most impactful things that has happened to me.

In this dream a Rinpoche and three Tibetan Buddhist monks come and visit me and they say 'hey you've got to come with us' so I find myself walking across a big square going into a multi storey skyscraper and getting into a lift. We go into a lift and we come up to a certain point and then the door opens. I look through and there's a red sky and as far as I can see there are millions and millions of people in various positions of copulation there is sexual activity in every possible modality.

This is just absolutely the the ultimate erotic mass orgy. Millions of people are all slithering and sliming about in semen having completely unrestrained sex, just bizarre. I'm looking out at it and I'm thinking 'must be heaven!' and at that point the Rinpoche behind coughs and mentally puts a thought in my mind that says 'look closer'. As I look closer I realise that these people are lost in a complete delusion, they can't remember coming into that place, there's no way out of it and whatever it is they're hoping for will never happen and there's no pleasure whatsoever. This is the consequence of a lifetimes' momentum of sexual fantasy and masturbatory energy. It's the consequence of desire, so when death came, the energy that was released went into sexual desire, these poor people ended up being drawn into this realm thinking that it was heaven just like I did and then actually realised that it wasn't at all because there's no way out and the sexual act is empty of any inherent pleasure there, it's a hell realm.

The Tibetan monks have spent their lives generating the power to liberate beings caught in this way. When I had my near death experience I also realised that many meditators and spiritual practitioners who do not achieve liberation in their lifetime will do so when they leave their bodies and when that incredible increase in sensitivity happens they will easily see what evaded them before and so become free. There will be lots of help when you die, don't get distracted, head for the light.

What is the Non-dual?

The Non-dual is a construct it's a concept, it's signifies a distinction. The way that the mind works is in duality as good, as bad, as yes and no, that's right, that's wrong, there's relative degrees of everything. Polarities and dualities and that's the way we mentally structure everything and even if we go down to a subatomic particle level we find that billions of times a second things are flashing on /off, on /off. So it could be said that duality is even the nature of nature.

The Nondual view is where there is no distinction between the seen, the seer and the seeing. The Non dual view is that which is underlying, penetrating, pervading all phenomena, Brahman. All things are made of the same cloth and have the same taste. Everything when broken down is made of the same substance. In a sleep dream we might dream of a diamond and a cloud and in that dream they seem to have different densities and be made of different substances, however on awakening we see that they were made of the same thing and that the appearance of their different densities was in fact an illusion, something that seemed to be real but was not. They were both made of the substance of dream. Everything in the sleep dream is equally unreal even though whilst dreaming we think of it as real.

The Nondual view points to the fact that here in the waking state we are under the same illusion, thinking that things are real and have inherent existence. When we transcend the duality of the intellects' operating system we see that everything is vibration in a unified field of vibration having no substantiality at all.

If things were real, each having substantial independent existence, they would emanate in such a way that everyone got them the same way. But nothing does, everyone gets everything differently and this is because we are the ones determining what things are and we all do it differently depending on the various causes and conditions that we have experienced.

There is no meaning that life emanates to us, any meaning we find is coming from us and everyones' meaning is slightly different.

The Nondual view sees what is the ground of being equally present everywhere, always. This field of inconceivable wonder that reveals nothing to be solid or fixed. A neutron coming from the sun hits the surface of the planet and passes right through the centre of the earth without loosing any momentum as it comes out the other side.

Time and space are held in this wondrous Awareness that never changes, moves yet somehow provides the intelligence that has everything in creation operating perfectly, from particles to galaxies.

The Nondual view sees that the notion of self and other is also an illusion. There is one being that has innumerable nodes of perception. We seem separate and different yet if for a moment we take all masks of identity off what remains is boundless having no edges. What is within and what is without are the same.

By experiencing this ground of being we transform our experience from it being an object to realising that we are it. In vedic terms we arrive at the seeing which is that "I am Brahman."

The Nondual view also reveals that we are not the doer of actions even though it really seems to be that we are. Actually we have never done anything. Take for example me writing this book: the idea to do it arose in my mind, the ideas contained herein also arose in my mind, the will to do it just appeared I did not make my will, the possibility of writing, printing and publishing was also not created by me. The consciousness that birthed the insights was also given, the insights just flashed into my mind which was also given. All I did and have ever done is witness all that occurs in the clearing of awareness, that includes witnessing consciousness states, thoughts which spontaneously arise, emotions, feelings and drama.

When after lifetimes of thinking I am the doer and I am the thinker, the witness finally emerges and my consciousness returns to its source and merges again with the ground of being which causes great joy and bliss, I realise that I am beyond the parts I have been playing in these countless lifetimes.

When I become very, very still perhaps during a Vipassana retreat, which is excellent for this, I mean really still, prolonged stillness, deep stillness putting everything down where you recognise your body is not solid there's no solidity to it at all, it's just a mass of sensations that give you the sense of weight and form. Then let that dissolve what's left is the sense of the perceiver, I'm perceiving this dissolution of my bodily awareness. Then there's a beautiful place where even the sense of a separate self observing phenomena that also melts and it is seen that that perception of a separate self was also a trick of consciousness with a very important purpose to create an objective platform from which this wonderful creation could see and know itself.

The final dualism is between the notion of the individual self and the all embracing over-self, when that finally dissolves it's like a raindrop hitting the ocean.

I had an incredible dream the other night which also talks speaks about this- in my dream I'm in a room and the great master Prem Rawat is there and there's three or four meditators and there's also the presence of two or three other people who are not in bodies anymore but I can hear them talking and thinking, I know that they're there, I can feel their vibe and in the same way the meditators that are there I can feel them I can feel their thinking, I can feel their vibe and also with the master I can feel him there. I can feel his radiant mind,I can feel him thinking and talking and vibrating we are in one vibration even though there appear to be separate beings, the presence is actually one and there's no separation between anything, between me and him or me and them. There's nowhere where I end or begin, I am just there as an expression of consciousness with no real substantially existing self. I realised that this is the experience that confirms the adage that"the mind of the master and the student are one". But actually the mind of the student and all life are also one! This is the Non dual view.

I am brought into being to witness the wonder of this life but in profound stillness of meditation even that separate self sense dissolves and there just this self-cognising awareness. This pure presence is completely ungraspable, undefinable, invisible having many of the properties of the sky, no edge, no centre everything happens in it, everything is pervaded by it.

As the Nondual view emerges and stabilises, suffering born of ignorance diminishes and lasting happiness unfolds.

Karma, dharma and drama

Dharma

Normally people think of dharma as being the teachings of somebody, the teachings of the Buddha, the buddha dharma but actually everything has a dharma. The dharma of fire is to burn, the dharma of water is to flow the dharma of an elephant is to be magnificent and unstoppable.

What is the dharma of a human? What is your dharma? You can get very particular about that because your dharma might be expressing your particular talents, but fundamentally what is the human dharma if the dharma of a fire is to burn, what is the dharma of a human?

What is our true purpose, what were we designed for? What is it that when we do it we are fully satisfied we are fully blissed out?

The dharma of a human being from my point of view is to love,to serve, to take care of life.

The mother knows that the dharma of a mother is

to take care of her children, when you're doing your dharma extraordinary qualities arise. I have seen some mothers who were anxious before they had their children or even women who come and see me and say 'no, no I'm never going to have a child, no I don't want one'. Often when you open that up and look at it a bit more deeply what's really there is low self worth or self hate and unworthiness.

The amazing thing about when we choose to fulfil our dharma, which in this case we're talking about being a mother, what I've seen is that incredible transformations happen and people who were selfish become so giving, they can give endlessly. They become fully loving and magnificent in the fulfilment of their dharma.

Following our dharma is the path to completion, is the path to being all that we can be and it's about loving, it's about caring. It's about being beyond self-cherishing where the motive behind all that we're doing is really just to look good and to feed our fabricated sense of self.

There is also another dharma unique to humans and that is to awaken to what truly is and revel in glory and gratitude. As far as we know no other living being can do that to the degree that we humans can.

Karma

Does a free person, does someone who has followed their dharma and realised the truth about the Self, the truth about the not self, the truth about the ego, does that one experience karma?

The 'I am presence', the witness, the one who witnesses my states of consciousness, the one who witnesses my thoughts, the one who witnesses my actions, does that one grow? No it doesn't.

Does the sky learn from the weather? Does the weather change the sky?

We can be the witness of karma unfolding in drama but we don't actually experience any.

Karma is a designation, is a super imposition, it's an interpretation, it's a map that has been invented through generations to describe inconceivable causality. The noble Buddha said 'dont 'bother talking about karma, it's way too complicated and if it's a thing it's not real'.

But we really are clear about it 'oh no there's definitely karma, your karma's gonna get you!' but it's really just a designation there isn't a substantially existing thing called karma.

People say karma is action and your actions create

your karma but all actions are empty how could they create karma?

It's not the action that creates the result but the beingness that that action comes from, the intent, the intention that that action comes from that generates the result that we get.

Two people can kill somebody, one a doctor is trying to save the life of someone in an intense surgery but fails to do so, the other is a murderer coming from evil intent, they both killed somebody. Obviously the karma is not the same, the result is not the same because the intention was different. It's the intention that creates the result or appears to.

Do we have to wait for our karma to burn out before we can be free?

No your karma in whatever state it is unfolds in perfect freedom. The weather no matter what it is, unfolds in a perfect sky which never changes.

Drama

In the drama of life we each have a part that we play.

'Oh I'm a man, I'm a woman, I'm undefined gender fluid', whatever it is. I'm this age, I've got this job, I've got opinions, I've got thoughts and I've got states of consciousness. All that makes up the part that I play in the drama of life.

But is that who I am? Am I the part that I play? All these conversations that are happening every day at the moment about gender, race and identity are addressing one question- who am I? This one we're looking at 'am I the part that I play'? My thoughts, which are part of the part that I play, supported by my internal thinking, is that who I am? Will I find myself in the part that I play, the identity I created in the drama of my life?

Am I who I think I am? Am I my thoughts, is that what determines who I am? My thoughts are unique ah so is that who I am, I'm my thoughts and am I my opinions? Perhaps my opinions are unique they're quite like everybody else's but they're all tweaked slightly differently, is that who I am, my opinions? Am I my karma, my unique karma no one has my karma is that who I am? I am the things that I've done that's what makes me unique, no one's done what

I've done. They've done similar but no one's done what I've done. Is that who I am and the answer is no, no, no, no that's not who we are that's all qualities of the part we play in the drama.

So what is the truth about who I am? Am I my qualities? I've got gifts, I can do this, I can't do that, the qualities and talents that I have is that who I am, that display themselves in the drama of my life is that who I am? No it's not! My misery, my unique misery, my unique sorrow, my unique capacity for upset is that who I, am no one had their heart broken like I did? Am I my pain my suffering is that who I am? No it's not that's all the quality and characteristics of the part you play in the drama!

That you witnessed, that you observed.

The witness sees but doesn't look, hears but doesn't listen. Totally impartial, unmoved and untouched by anything witnessed.

We seek identity and the resolution of our ongoing existential identity crisis in drama by modifying the part we play. Thinking that if we had more of this less of that we would be happy or if we could get others to validate our current version of ourself that would fix the subtle sense of disease within. We join in the consensus view and adopt perspectives like 'you are what you got" 'the more you have the better you are"'you are how much power you have" but even when we are successful in getting these things there is no end to the inner unknowing. So we start suppressing our anxieties, we start suppressing our fears the next thing we know our hearts have hardened and we can't feel the love and so we live locked in a mental reality.

If you just stop doing all the things that are the constituent parts of the part you play in the movie of your life, if you stop doing all of that, stop acting for a moment, stop thinking for a moment, stop being fascinated by and caught up in your states of consciousness for a moment and let be what is.

What is left that is the Self!

The fabulous inconceivable simplicity of who I am. How amazing it is to be this freedom that you always are at the source,as you get it then it becomes much easier to have longer and longer periods where you are effortlessly present just by remembering it.

People don't like letting go of identifying as their mind because they think that it decodes and interprets what is happening accurately and without it they would be lost.

But you have to really see how much misery and pain and suffering has come through your association with your mind. Thinking 'I am the thinker' no you're not, you're far more wonderful than that! Thinking is pretty incredible, it's amazing look at all that's been created from it now we've got a machine that will think for itself, the ai as we speak it's learning itself without being told what is more incredible than that we might ask!

What is the great final ultimate secret of life?

The view from the mountain top, the ultimate view for you? Even if you only have this in a lifetime for a moment you are very, very, very, blessed.

What is that ultimate view? All there is, is love.

I was dreaming and then I was awakened and when I awakened I realised all there was is love.

We can come so far from that and then we suffer. Our suffering can be measured by the distance we are from knowing that and being that. Being at a place where even when breathing you're breathing love, you can give love, taking love, giving love, drawing love, sending love, receiving love or just being a lover in a field of love loving.

A little time in presence can activate a process of Awakening like a certain amount of sunlight will activate the plants growth and if all the conditions are good it will blossom it will release it fragrance it will absorb wonderful energies from the sun naturally automatically and effortlessly.

Karma dissolves in the light of your awakening. The momentums we've been traveling on as a waveform from a beginning to an end, traveling through time and space in a continuum, then life directs us to self-observe and we find we have a different mode of being, we break down into presence, into particle presence, hovering and being in this now, fully present as presence.

In this now there isn't anything that was before unless we go and bring it in this now is always pure, this now is always clear, this now is always profound peace and silence. It doesn't matter what's going on in the drama this peace remains even when it's noisy, this clarity is there even when confusion is observed, this love holds life even when we feel hate.

So how do we get there? The heart is the guide we think our mind is the guide, we think we know it all already, we think our understanding is realisation. It's not just a matter of understanding something you have to realise it by experiencing it directly which we can do now by simply seeing what's here.

When you realise what's being said it will transform your relationship to your life, to your feelings, to the past. It will transform your relationship. You will naturally start being kinder, you will naturally start being more generous, you will naturally not be entertaining so much judgment you will naturally become disenchanted with opinions, you will naturally become more bored by gossip. You will be drawn towards stillness, you'll be drawn towards nature, you'll be drawn towards caring.

How to stay as Presence

There are two basic ways that a human being is in the waking state. It's actually the same with everything, all phenomena.

Either we are appearing as a wave form or we are appearing as particle presence. When we're appearing as a wave form we are traveling from the beginning to the end our life, birth to death and we are traveling as a character, as a person with a body and a story supported by internal dialogue.

As long as you have a body you will be playing a part in a story and you will be a character in that story. Even if you sat in a cave you would still be playing the part of the guy sitting in the cave and that's the waveform but what science has shown us is that anytime we observe what we're observing is changed by observation of it and so if we observe ourself then that brings us into particle presence. Suddenly we're not traveling from somewhere going to somewhere, we're right here in this moment as particle presence.

What does that mean it means that we begin to realise that this sense of solidity, this sense of weight, this sense of matter it's actually nothing more than a sense. It's not actually the truth about what this body is. When we come into particle presence we become an energy field and our hands, bones, thoughts, feelings and everything about us is vibrating at different frequencies.

The question then is if we are a waveform being a personality, having a drama, how do we break out of that and come into presence?

The feeling of being alive right here now and it's incredible, once you have a clear distinction of what presence is. It's a feeling that you are alive within that somehow within you is not bones and organs and lungs and bits of sort of machinery but somehow within you it's energy, a subtler part of you and you are alive, you can feel yourself vibrating, you can feel that you are in fact energy. That is what it means to be alive as presence, to be actually right here now, not in a fantasy of the mind, not in a sense of a gross material body as an emanating being.

As you go into that you feel it expand as you wake into it awakens and blossoms and blossoms more until you become intensely peaceful and your mind has become quiet and you realise that you're centreing in the heart with your breath which also becomes quieter and quieter until you come to a complete standstill that's the heart of presence.

The heart of every moment is pure presence, your presence isn't somewhere more than another place it's the same everywhere. Pure presence doesn't come and go but our access our experience of it that does come and go.

So how to return to it, from my perspective, I recognise it as a path of remembrance it seems that that we are born and the default place where we live is as a wave form, as a character in a play. You're a mother, you're a father your brother, your a sister, you're a lawyer, a doctor or whatever that is supported by our thinking, the internal dialogue making comment on everything, telling you how you are telling you what everything is, defining everything.

All that is needed once you have established clearly what presence is and one way to do that is to find someone who is established as presence and let them point you to it. Once you've got that clear then you can return on a thought, on a breath and then everything in nature you realise reflects that and is that, so anytime you look at anything in nature presence starts to come. You start to steady your gaze, quiet down, relax your breath and presence starts to unfold.

You take a breath and relax the tension and come into being, coming into presence and coming into being are the same.

A thought, you remember something that

somebody has said and that thought can put you into it again. It's a path of remembrance, it's not the default feeling as soon as your attention on it goes, it goes.

Maybe further down the line you might remain in presence, you might even recognise yourself as presence but certainly in the beginning stages if you lose your attention to it, it goes and you're back in your mind making judgments, having thoughts, developing opinions, thinking about the past, thinking about the future which is all to do with maintaining the character that you play in the waveform aspect of your existence.

But as soon as you self observe again you come back into presence.

When you come back into presence you don't lose the character that you were playing, you can still come back to it but it's just at this moment you're in the modality of being fully present as presence.

Presence shows you that you are whole, you're not becoming whole, you are your presence. It doesn't evolve, it can't be lost stolen, it doesn't diminish, you right here right now. The reason why it doesn't diminish, can't be lost, can't be stolen and it can't be stained is because your individual sense of yourself as presence, which seems to emanate from a point, actually is a ripple in a vast ocean of pure omnipresence.

There isn't really any difference between the sense that you have 'I am' in that pure, beautiful, still place and the ocean that it's happening in, which you could call the great Self.

First to remember is what brings you back, remember who you are, remember that who you think you are which is coming out of your internal dialogue and coming out of the past that is not who you are, that's just who you 'think' you are.

So many things you thought they were a certain way but actually you find out they weren't that way at all and never more so than with oneself. Who you think you are it's not who you are, there's something wrong with who you think you are, the character you've created yourself to be, it has fears and phobias, it has complexes and unresolved issues. Fortunately that isn't who you are, that's very temporary and changes all the time, it's never the same twice, you never appear to yourself the same way twice.

When you return to presence you can have the possibility of understanding that your thoughts arise of their own accord, you have been thinking that 'I am the thinker' but actually what is seen after a while is that your thoughts arise of their own accord given by who your being that life is in any one moment. So you remember presence and you come back, you stay in presence by remembering that it's possible, by steadying your focus into anything natural, or your breath.

What happens when you look at something without blinking? Prove it just try it, look at a flower, look at the sky and don't blink. Calm down and you'll notice that certain things start to happen, you'll notice that your breathing changes, it drops and releases and then if you don't think you'll notice that it just gets lighter and lighter and that you can almost see the luminosity of presence vibrating.

The presence that is out here is non-different to the presence in here, a field of energy, a field of consciousness, a field of wisdom not as concepts but wisdom as just resting in the presence of what is. Bathe your mind in presence, bathe your heart and release everything into presence.

The mind wants to know how to do it, it will never understand but if you want to you will as much as you want to.As much as you do, you'll want it more and as much as you want more you'll be given more. It's not difficult neither is it easy. Presence is where you realise the truth of what reality is. The truth about yourself, truth about the Universe the truth about life and death,the truth about what this actually is.

So choose presence, choose to remember and live in that remembrance. Presence turns into Love. Choose Love.

The Difference Between Understanding and Realisation

"Understanding is the booby prize." Werner Erhardt

Understanding and realisation is a great distinction to make. The fact that you understand the mechanics of love doesn't make you a lover, The fact that you understand the mechanics of spirituality, the nature of the self, the laws of karma does not make you truly spiritual. The fact you understand the laws of manifestation doesn't make you able to manifest, there is another element that needs to be in place.

In order for something to actually impact and transform you have to 'get it'. There are in fact two stages, the first stage is you understand the concepts that contain the realisation the second stage is that you get it you get it ontologically, you get it on the level of being such that it actually transforms who you're being that life is, so that it turns up differently.

For example if you understand the nature of the Self, you understand that it's not your persona that's not who you are, that it's not your psychological self either that is the Self.You understand that. It is beneficial just even knowing that but it won't make any real difference in the way that you behave or how life occurs. But if you really 'get it', if you really see directly, if you have an insight then that will transform your behaviour. You have realised the concept that you previously understood. There has to be a direct insight had by the person them self on the level of being, into the true nature of what it is and then that allows you to transform naturally and effortlessly.

There's two ways that we learn one is by deducing and processing information and the other is by direct insight. Direct insight is seeing things as they actually are and that isn't necessarily using your mind in the sense of creating thoughts and conceptual constructs about it, it's actually just seeing it. Being present to what is IS transforming.

Just understanding is not transforming, people think that the understanding is it but it isn't, if it hasn't changed you, if it hasn't transformed you, if it hasn't freed you. Often people do a lot of research and get an understanding but do not get the fruit, they don't realise it and consequently there is no transformation then they can become cynical.

What you realise becomes you and yours, what you understand you can forget because it's in the memory stored away as concepts, what you understand you can lose what you understand can be wrong. What you realise can't be wrong what you realise is beyond right and wrong. What you realise is truth, the way things are coming from insight. Realisation is only partially stored in the memory and mostly contributes to awakening. What is realised or seen in this sense can not be unseen.

Understanding is like a menu but you need to eat the food which is realising, it's like a map but you need to take the journey. I would suggest do not rest with just understanding it's not enough, it doesn't do it it's almost like understanding is the minds version of realisation.

Someone else's realisation can only become your understanding but their realisation can inspire you and show you that it is possible. When a person speaks from a place of realisation it's different to when someone speaks from their understanding. Something powerful can be transmitted that can inspire direct cognition in you. No one can give another realisation. There is something to realise that will transform who you're being that this life is such that you stabilise in a happy calm, fascinating, joyous place. You can realise what the Self actually is for yourself, they did it so can you!

Understanding is made of conceptual constructs which do help, it's exciting to get a new concept or to get a new view. When your understanding becomes condensed into a new refined understanding that's exciting but it still it weighs and wears off, like getting a new car, it's great for a bit and then it's just a new car and the shine wears off.

The cynical ones are cynical because they confused understanding with realisation they understood it all but it still didn't transform them so they know of it but have not seen it, there is suppressed disappointment and resentment, they think they know better and it becomes a layer of frozenness over their heart.

Realisation is different, realisation is to strike gold, so realise for yourself, unfold the gift of this life, unfold what's in your heart see what is vibrating throughout the moment directly.

What is the Awakening?

The awakening is something incredible it's a wonderful possibility that can occur in anyone's life. Normally there are three states that we are in, we are either in deep dreamless sleep or we're dreaming or we're awake. Now most people don't think of the waking state as having degrees so you're either awake or you're dreaming or asleep but there is the possibility of looking at it that you can be awake and kind of dreaming you're awake. In other word's not fully awake, there are degrees of wakefulness.

What do you experience when you are fully awake that's different from what is normally felt when you're a little bit awake? Most people when they're awake they know they're awake because they can hear themselves think and they see stuff unfold in front of them, when you're fully awake you feel presence, you can feel that energy.

So the awakening is when you come into the fourth state which presents itself initially as the feeling of presence. Presence is when your normal sense of physicality of solidity of your body starts to subtly shift and you realise that actually what you are made of is energy vibrating at different frequencies. Matter is energy.

In meditation many people come into that realisation that actually there is only energy and in that place where there's only energy there is also peace, clarity and selflessness.

By accessing Presence eventually a natural process of Awakening can get triggered whereby what it was that one used to identify with, the ego, the persona, the part I played in the movie of my life, starts to shift and then quietness comes above your shoulders. There isn't a sense of a character in there, it goes spacious and it's almost as if the sky reaches down to your shoulders.

As you continue in your attention to presence you become presence rather than having it as an object. Identifying as presence, the psychological self that you were identified as, the broken one, the wounded one, the unintegrated one you realise that that was just a version of yourself that your mind gave you and your mind didn't realise that beyond all that, prior to that, prior to the persona, prior to the psychological self is something absolutely wonderful- your presence. As you are no longer pouring all your attention into the psychological self it starts to disassemble and great chunks of it just fall away.

When we arrive as pure presence we still have the sense that we are an individual entity quietened down, simplified just pure presence emanating, a point of reference and a heart from which the universe is perceived. Then going even more deeply into that there comes a point where even that hub is seen to be a play of consciousness and that dissolves and then all there isa mass of self cognising presence, pure awareness.

The goal is to walk through the door to have the awakening, to see that there's something prior to the personality, to see that there's something before the psychological self, you were before you started to think and develop a sense of who you are as an ego, you were there, you've always been there. You as pure presence do not evolve, it never changes, each time you return to pure presence, to that awakened state it's exactly the same, spacious, clear, peaceful and loving.

The awakening is when you're fully alive, no part is sleeping and then this presence, this moment, any moment regardless of what the circumstances of that moment are, any moment has this luminous quality to it. The heart of any moment regardless of the circumstances is deep, deep, peace. The heart of any moment is this beautiful awakened awareness.

You realise I am that which I've been looking at and there is the beautiful awakening and it's endless it has no limit. Even though it's always the same each time you return to it, it's always fresh and we can depend on that, we don't have to plan everything out, we don't have to think everything through, we can rely on our awakeness, we can rely on that pure presence ,we can rely on life.

This is a path of wonder and joy where there's enough clarity and enough space mentally to be able to see the very heaven that is this earth and also to see the incredible opportunity that we have by virtue of the fact we're alive. There is a mass awakening happening, everybody no matter what they do or have done or what ever they believe can be part of it simply because they're alive.

Choose Freedom!

When you choose freedom you don't have to know what you're talking about just choose freedom! I choose that whatever else was going to happen in my life, whatever else I'm going to do, whatever other responsibilities I've got, I choose freedom.

Actually I choose to be freedom, I am freedom, what freedom is. There's no limit, there's no obstruction there's no block, no edge, just freedom, spaciousness, bellowing joy.

Freedom from the tyranny of mind thinking that I am the thinker'. All the pain, all the suffering without exception has come from thinking that 'I am the thinker' that is the cause of slavery to your mind.

Choosing freedom will bring the realisation that thoughts just spontaneously arise. I don't have to be concerned, they arise in my freedom. The freedom that I am, it doesn't come and go and it doesn't change. Freedom is the space within which everything arises. Nothing makes freedom freedom there's no condition that has to be there for freedom to be freedom it's already complete.

Problem is we've got our heads where the Sun isn't shining! We've got our heads filled with thoughts and are desperately thinking trying to get a handle on what it all is and who I am. Yet what has come from asking your thoughts who am I? What has come is the idea that something is wrong, we don't know quite what! Is it something to do with your mother, your parents, your upbringing, your sister, your brother, what happened, the desperate trauma, the taboos, the sex thing, all of that stuff there is something wrong and that's why I am not good enough or happy. That's what comes when you ask your mind Who am I and what's happening? Then you're limited in this tiny box of what life can be and your possibility shrinking to nothing and then you have to ask the TV or the computer or somebody else what it is my life is for.

There's no joy there, there's not really love there, you might get a little bit of admiration, people admire you for your sufferings, your tenacity.

However if you choose freedom then completely separate from the conceptual world something starts to happen, something starts becoming apparent and we shift away from an egocentric mind dominated thinking and we unfold into a different place and there's all kinds of people, situations and things that can work as reflectors and pointers. When we're ready for that everything can reflect you to freedom if you're there to see.

But we say to ourselves 'I'm not good enough, it

might exist, but I'm not good enough, nothing really good has ever happened to me' and we identify like that with mediocrity and we don't have a space where something wonderful can happen.

Fortunately it doesn't really matter because nothing can stop freedom coming because it's already here and you can see it, you just get it, 'oh my god I've been farting in a field of flowers surrounded by the most incredible fragrance!' Freedom is the ocean that we're floating in and when we become fully quiet all there is is freedoms glorious song reflected in everything.

You don't have to be clever, you don't have to be educated, you just have to recognise that you really want it and that what's been going on is not what is really on offer. You know this is it not it no, there's something incredible waiting for you this freedom.

The act of choosing is not like deciding for freedom which is a convoluted mental process and like other convoluted mental processes doesn't really do anything but choosing freedom happens when your flower is just about to break open into blossom and it arises in you and you just choose freedom, you agree with everything life is saying and you choose freedom and that choice reconfigures and finally tunes and activates the most wonderful blossoming in your heart and in your consciousness and then your consciousness lifts up and touches into awareness itself and there is the sea of the greatest freedom.

You could be 93 and today is the day, you could be 18 and today is the day or any age in between it's got nothing to do with how old you are. It's a wonderful conspiracy, it's what you didn't know you didn't know, it's the ultimate conspiracy behind all conspiracies which is that you should be freedom. So many great people have said 'if you wake up there's something amazing' so you have a little faith like 'okay I choose to wake up, I choose freedom, whoever's out there, whatever it is, whatever can do it, help me because I'm not free and I want to be free!' and when that is coming from your authentic thirst, that real place inside, the universe goes 'so we've been waiting for you that's all we have been waiting for! Okay get ready because here it comes and once one gift from heavenly realms is received, the next one comes following right after and the next one and the next one and the next one. All you've got to do is keep receiving, keep receiving and the next thing you know your whole life has transformed. You've got the same body but the internal landscape has shifted and changed and you are with your breath and your mind has become quiet and then the gratitude starts flowing 'thank you, thank you, thank you'.

There is no reason why, you did nothing except allow it to unfold by choosing. So good luck with that, choose freedom now!

There is no way that you are the sky is not blue!

Most of us spend a large amount of time thinking about who we are. We think that our personality characteristics and our behaviour and meanings that we've created from how we appeared in our lives that is who we are. And depending on how we are feeling in any one moment that will determine how we see ourselves.

We can sometimes judge ourselves very harshly and often self hate even emerges and then it's not a good experience living in that psychologically inspired identity.

If through making bad choices or being run by unconscious urges and compulsions we have made mistakes which we now feel guilty about or shameful of then this also makes living in psychological identity not a happy place.

As we grow older the self-made construct of who we get ourselves to be gets more solidified until we really do think that is who we are.

Typically we will have it that there is something wrong with us due to experiences of childhood traumas that have occurred in our life.

Also at the same time we will be thinking that there is something special about us and that in some way we are better than others. This sense of being special balances out the opposite sense of being not good enough.

From early childhood we asked 'who am I?' and the answer came from parents, teachers and from our own often misinformed thinking. Many people settle for this version of themselves and so live most of their lives just above the threshold of conscious suffering. As this identity is housed and generated in a world of thought and is just a construct there is little possibility of real joy, love and peace.

The fact is that the only place you exist is in this now, and present in this Now, there is no way that you are. This means that where life is actually happening there is no way that you are. For there to be a way that you are you would need to go into memory and conditioning from the past and drag it in to this fresh new now.

Is there a way that the sky is? Does it change, does it accumulate identity as the weather passes through it?

There is no way that the sky is, the sky is separate from its content and it would not be correct to identify the sky with its content. The sky is not blue, that blue is created when the sunlight reaches

Earth's atmosphere and is scattered in all directions by all the gases and particles in the air. Blue light is scattered more than the other colours because it travels as shorter, smaller waves. So we can see that there is no way that the sky is yet it is definitely there.

Likewise our states of consciousness, our changing sense of identity, our thoughts, our feelings and even the drama of our lives can all be considered as weather happening in our sky like awareness.

Who I am must be the constant thing about me which is the witness, the observer, the one who listens to me think, who witnesses my consciousness states yet is unassociated with them and unaffected by them. Just as the sky remains unaffected by all the storms and weather that passes through it. So there is no way that I am, I am a clearing in which all life takes place.

If you have understood what I am saying then it is a thing of great joy because it points to complete freedom.

To be in the world of "there is no way that I am" is to be spaciousness, clarity, joy and unbounded freedom!

I can stop trying to fix myself, I can stop trying to figure out who I am because now I see there is no way that I am!!

Who I am being that I am gives me how I appear to myself but it is an appearance only and is witnessed.

It becomes clear that I am not the part I play in this lifetime drama just as I am not my body, I am also not my thoughts or the thinker, I am the one that dispassionately witnesses all that happens on all levels in my life, and as such there is no way that I am.

As there is no way that I am, I never change, I do not evolve or get affected in anyway by the experiences that I witness in my life.

The realisation that there is no way that I am is a portal to the possibility of being that all there is is love...

Chapter 4

Meetings With Remarkable Men

Professor Miagyi

I was riding on my scooter around the back roads behind Ram Jhula in Rishikesh, India. I wanted to sit and have a quiet smoke, I had tried one place in the jungle but as soon as I sat down police came.

Warning me that there were elephants in the area and that I should not sit here alone.I was thinking about my guru's brother Satpal Maharaj.

I knew that he was the minister of tourism in that

state and I was thinking casually 'if he really was a cosmic being he would hear me and give me a place to sit where I can do my sadhana'.

Literally at that moment a baba jumps out from the side of the road and starts waving at me, so I pull my scooter over to see what he wants and he comes up to me with a book in his hand and opens the book and points to the author who is none other than Satpal Maharaj - the man who I was just thinking about! I found this astonishing then after we had talked about practice and realisation for a while he asked my name "Tim" I replied to which he responded "Tim Williams?" I never did figure out how he knew my name it was really very strange.

He tells me that there is a cave up a path beyond a chai shop in the jungle where I could go and meditate in peace. So we go and have a chai and then I left him and take my scooter up the path to the little ashram where the caves were.

I decided to walk up past the caves, beyond is a waterfall, flowers and garlands a place of great beauty. I find an area and prepare a place for sitting. After my smoke I entered a beautiful and deep meditation. After some time I become aware of a voice saying to me 'just listen to the river with unbroken attention and you will come into a more profound state.' So I did this and found myself realising that the key to meditation, going into deeper states, is to maintain longer and longer moments of unbroken concentration. The sound of the bubbling river was becoming more ecstatic the longer I listened to it.

I sat for about an hour and then I opened my eyes and I saw a baba with dreadlocks and another man dressed in ordinary clothes washing down by the river.

The baba waved and the man in ordinary clothes came over to talk to me. He asked did I hear him talking to me during my meditation? I said yes I did, he then asked would I like to sit with him tomorrow? I said I would and we arranged to meet the next day. His English was not very good but he kept saying 'Mount Kailash' and showed me a picture on his phone of a four armed deity whose name I did not know but he kept tapping it making sure that I had seen it.

I went back down to town feeling excited about all the synchronicities that had unfolded that afternoon, it was amazing to me.

I came back the next day and soon after I had sat down he appeared with a meditation mat which he placed near to mine and then started breaking up some twigs which I think he was going to use to count mantras with. When he had done this he said 'are you ready?' and I closed my eyes. He started chanting a mantra the only word I knew in the mantra was 'Agoura'. Soon I was having vivid visions I saw a great yogi standing almost naked wearing a red and gold cloak holding a great trident, symbol of Shiva.

After that I saw clearly the sacred Mount Kailash and found myself travelling towards it, still sitting in my meditation posture but being able to fly through the sky! On the side of the mountain there is a long vertical fissure, as I approached it I saw that there were other yogis coming and going using this great crack in the mountain as an entrance so I flew on in.

As soon as I entered the mountain on my right side I saw the statue of a four armed deity exactly like the one he had showed me on his phone. I could not see the face of the deity but I knew to bow so I did. It then came to me that I had further access privileges so I travelled on into the mountain until I came upon Lord Shiva and Parvati wonderful luminous, loving light beings, sitting on a throne. I did not stay long in fact I think I became unconscious before I left them there was so much light and presence.

On my return I opened my eyes and for a moment I clearly saw Mount Kailash in the next valley!

I asked the gentleman who had facilitated this subtle body journey what his name was he looked at me and smiled and said 'Professor Miyagi' which I thought was really funny! (Professor Miagyi is the sensei of Karate Kid in the films of that name!)

This man clearly had powers one of which was telepathy, we talked at a distance without speaking and he knew about it. Also he had the power to lift me out of my body and take me into another world.

I told him about the great Baba that I had seen standing with his trident and he told me that it was Mastaram Baba who used to live in this cave and was very highly respected by all who knew him but now he had left his body. I knew that he was now living in some kind of Shiva heaven.

Later, quite by chance I got to sit with Satpal Maharaj the minister of tourism for Uttrakand state, as he gave a spiritual discourse about the power of unbroken focus. Such is incredible India!

Chuck Wein

I had driven with some friends to Los Angeles from Florida and we were living in Hollywood. I was meeting all kinds of strange people, one night I went into a coffee shop 2:30 in the morning and a man called me over. He had a very ordinary appearance, middle aged wearing a clean white shirt. 'Sit down, I want to show you something.' I sat down intrigued by his approach he put his hands out across the table and said 'take my hands I want to show you the love and compassion of Mother Mary, the Divine Mother'.I took his hands in mine and gazed into his eyes as I did I experienced an energy surge coming from him and his look became very loving and compassion seemed to pour from his eyes, after a while tears silently rolled down his cheeks. I was really shocked by the feeling of love, it was not personal he was simply channeling the divine Mother.

He said he had worked in a coal mine all his life in Pittsburgh, the one day Mother Mary came to him and ever since he could transmit her love and compassion.

Another time I was walking down Hollywood Boulevard at midnight when a Chevrolet pulls up beside me and the guy in it says for me to get in. There was something about him and the way he said it that made me feel safe to get in so I did.

He was very bright and cool and I told him of some of the experiences I had been having he said "I know, here comes another!" We went to his apartment on Sunset Boulevard and he offered me a joint of marijuana mixed with damiana, a powerful herb used by shamen the world over. I started to feel energy rising and my consciousness expanding. We stood up and looked into each other's eyes, as I looked his eyes went deep turquoise and he started to talk to me in an unknown but familiar language, what he was saying stirred my heart deeply and I found myself replying to him in the same language! We embraced as if we were long lost brothers who had found each other again.

He told me to sit on a throne like carved chair, so I did as I relaxed something shifted in me and I went off not returning until I sat in the same chair again two weeks later!

I went to Venus which is a spiritual planet of highly evolved beings who vibrate in love and have light bodies that can assume as much density as they desire. I remember visiting the most beautiful temple in the middle of which was a violet flame about 20 feet tall shining a spiritual light and vibrating the atmosphere around it. As I approached it the violet flame parted to reveal a pure white light core in which was written the words 'I AM'. The flame reached into my heart. There were also great halls filled with wondrous beings doing all kinds of exotic spiritual practice the like of which I had never seen.

During the time I was 'off planet 'my body and life functioned normally it was only a subtle part of me that was on Venus. One day I walked into a shop in Hollywood and found a Venusian/English dictionary! It was a very strange time.

I visited Chuck a few times during this period and he told me that he was a wizard. He was a friend of Andy Warhol (which later research found to be true) and also made the film Rainbow Bridge with Jimi Hendrix who he knew well and who he declared was not from this world and was also a wizard of a different kind. He told me about my function and aptitudes which he believed were being activated.

He was also a man with telepathic powers and had a strange unstoppability about him. I heard much later when I returned to Los Angeles thinking to reconnecr with him that he had died mysteriously in a house fire.

Devraha Baba

Sri Devraha Baba, an Indian Siddha saint was possibly one of the most extraordinary people I have ever met as he was reputed to be over 300 years old.

It was 1989 and I was attending the Maha Kumbha Mela, an epic and vast gathering of Hindus at Allahabad where the Ganga, the Yamuna and the underground Saraswati rivers meet. Reckoned to be the most sacred place of all. Tens of millions of people came to take a sacred bath in this sacred spot at the right moment over a five week period.

I had heard that there was a baba who was supposed to be over 300 years old who was attended to by Prime Ministers, heads of state and other dignitaries so I decided to go and see him.

As I approached there was a huge crowd gathering round a small house on stilts. Leaning over the balcony was the baba himself. He seemed to have very thick dark skin, deep set eyes and a beautiful golden radiance. He wore only a deer skin, it appears that he could not straighten his back but he seemed very energised and present.

I made my way to the front of the crowd in an

attempt to ask him a question so that I might engage with him. He did not speak English so my question was put to one of his helpers who then translated for the Baba. The question was 'when may a man say I am God?' He looked down into my eyes and when I looked into his eyes it appeared that he was coming from miles away from a point deep inside himself.

His answer was delivered in a very intense and rapid manner.

According to the Vedas there are several things that have to be present before a man can say he is a divine incarnation. For example he must be born at an auspicious time, also he must have auspicious marks on his body, there were other qualifications which I have now forgotten. I felt a very powerful connection to this ancient human there was no doubt he was very, very old but his mind was encyclopaedic, very sharp and precise.

Apparently he ate very little every day, bathed in the Ganga, liked to drink milk and preferred to be off the ground as much as possible.

As I left the crowd I ran into Claudio, an old friend of mine, who told me that the day before he had come to see the great man and the Baba had seen him and started pointing at him and telling his aides to come and bring my friend to him. Claudio said that the Baba ordered his immediate initiation as he was a disciple of the Baba in a previous lifetime.

He went on to say that now he was staying in the Devraha Baba camp and that if I wanted I could stay with him. So we went to the tent which was also occupied by another Baba with long dreadlocks. This man was very different, proud and superior but welcoming so I put my bag down and went off with Claudio, my Italian friend, to see the extraordinary sights.

When I came back I opened by bag and realised that things had changed inside, alarmed I looked for my passport which had my three £50 notes in it. I found the passport but the money had gone.

At that moment the Baba and Claudio came in I told them what had happened the Baba said if I wanted he could ask Baba Ji (a discarnate yogi) if he knew where the money was. So he sat down crossed his legs into the full lotus, adjusted his hair and opened a bag by his side. He pulled out the top half of a human skull which he touched respectfully to his forehead. Then taking it in one hand like a telephone, he put it to his ear:

' BabaJi, oh BabaJi are you there?"

"Hallo, hallo, ah Babaji yes the Englishman says he has lost his money do you know where it is? Ah Ok, acha, Ok thank you Baba!"

He then told me that the money has gone and some would return by sunset. So me and Claudio went off till sunset. When I returned I saw that two of the £50 notes had been returned but still one was missing. I told the Baba to please get Babaji on the line again and find out where the other note was or there would be trouble. So the baba got his skull out and contacted Babaji again to enquire about the other note. We could hardly keep a straight face!

The baba told us that Babaji said the other note will not be returning due to complicated reasons of karma.I responded by saying that if it did not come back within an hour I would speak to Devraha Baba himself to see if he had a better connection!

The skull baba did not believe I would do that. There was clearly a major cultural disconnect happening between us!

When nothing happened by an hour after sunset I went to see the great Baba.It was dark now and I was able to speak to the translator who told my story to the old Baba. His response was to call the skull baba over and then for both of us to wait in front of his hut on stilts. We sat thirty feet away from each other with Devraha Baba in between for about twenty minutes.

There were strong psychic vibes as the skull baba was having his bluff called. After a while I was called over to the hut and handed a bag of money mostly in 2 rupee notes.I left, the judgement had been called in my favour as it should have been. I never found out what happened to the skull baba.

A couple of years after this Devraha Baba finally left his body.

Bluey

I was quite young when I met Bluey. I was at a small festival in England and someone had given me some speed I was feeling uncomfortable so I decided to chant Hare krishna. As I did I gathered more and more momentum tell I was doing it incredibly fast and the people in the tent with me all fell asleep as the chanting reached it's crescendo an image of Lord Krsna appeared on the screen above the stage. At that moment I heard some shouting so I got up and ran over to the Release tent.

The Release tent was a place where people having bad trips on LSD or other substances could go and find support. When I got in there it appeared that everybody was on something and there was pandemonium. People freaking out and screaming and shouting in a in a whirlpool of chaos. I was trying to calm it all down and sort it all out when I felt a hand on my shoulder I turned round and there was a native American Indian wearing a black hat with a turquoise and silver band. He looked into my eyes and said 'don't do anything, let it all be'.

I relaxed and as I did the whirlpool came to an end and calm was restored. Bluey seemed to know me in a most unusual way, he was extremely psychic and captured my interest by telling me what was in my mind and things that I had done. He appealed to my ego by telling me that I had some function in a magical sense, that I was a transmitter and whatever I focused on the multiplied. I was impressed he said that he was a native American Shaman and that when he was young he had been taken by the CIA who put him through a series of intense tests to try and find out what exactly his power was. Apart from this he told me very little about himself.

The festival ended and I returned to Brighton where I was living in a flat with several other meditators. The following day after my arrival I ran into Bluey and it turned out that he had just rented a flat just over the roof from the one that I was in.

He told me that I could choose what I amplified and that he was going to give me a seed to see if I wanted it.

That afternoon I was meditating and I slightly drifted off and I felt a presence then something popped into my heart chakra. As the days unfolded I started to feel a dark power develop within. One of its most obvious manifestations was the power to seduce women knowing exactly how to be in order to capture their full attention. All kinds of synchronicity started happening and each day I felt this dark power grow within me.

Bluey started coming into our flat and ingratiating himself with the others who all thought he was great. However I started having doubts about what he was really up to. I began to feel that he wanted to use me for something. So I cast the I Ching, an ancient Chinese Oracle, to see if it could give me any clarity and it did. It said an evil man has entered your circle the others do not see him as he is it is your responsibility to get him out!

So one night I thought if he really is dark he won't be able to handle listening to the satsang (spiritual discourse) from the Guru because that is so bright and light. So we asked him to come to a satsang and as he couldn't really say no, he came and by the end of the satsang he was very, very agitated and uncomfortable, like a Demon that had spent too long in the light.

We all went home altogether but I knew that the confrontation between him and me was going to happen tonight. Everyone left and I confronted him and told him that he was no longer welcome in our circle and that whatever his intentions for me were they were not going to happen. He became angry and said 'you've got nothing, I am one with the power!' I told him to get out or I'll call the police he said go on,' there go onto the balcony and you will see'.So I went to the balcony and looked down and low and behold there were two police, I called out but they appeared to be oblivious of my shouting. Bluey said 'don't worry they're not going to hear you however loud you shout', and they didn't hear me they just walked on.

So then I got a bunch of incense and I lit it placed it on the gurus alter and then turned on the Guru speaking. From that point he started to lose power became very angry but the game was over he had been exposed and banished he could not take the vibration of the guru and so left with his tail between his legs and I never saw him again.

However that seed of darkness was still in me what to do? As it happened a month or so later I went to America to see the guru at a large festival near Disneyland. One afternoon during the festival the guru was speaking and I became a little drowsy and lost contact with him drifting off. Suddenly he's shouting very loudly and his voice is like a bolt of energy that hits my heart and blasts the dark seed away! Suddenly I'm very awake and tears of devotion well up.

Shortly after he finished the band came on and played some music, the master stood up and started dancing raising his hands in the air, he danced the dance that symbolises the victory of the light and in my heart I knew why. Such is the glory of the Guru.

Joey

I had arrived in Toronto by flying from the UK with no ticket and a lot of grace.

It happened because I figured that if my guru had invited me then there must be a way to fulfil on that, regardless of whether I had any money or not. So I went to the airport and found a ticket envelope which I flashed as I went through. Then I came to a boarding gate and there was a kerfuffle going on it was Paul McCartney boarding another plane so in the confusion I got under the rope and went down the ramp to the bus that was to take us to the plane.

Inside the bus I saw my friend so I sat next to him. He was very shocked to see me I asked him to give me his ticket and for him to keep his boarding card and I would say I lost my boarding card. It all worked brilliantly and they reissued the boarding card. So we both boarded luckily the plane was not full so seating was not a problem. We taxied to the end of the runway, I was listening Ode to Joy as we hurtled down the runway when I looked out of the window and the engine was on fire!!

There was the sudden shudder of full brakes and abort of the takeoff and a great noise as the plane shook and then finally came to a standstill.

We were safe, the fire was put out but we all had to get off and onto a bus and back to the airport. Any way it all worked out fine and eventually we got to Toronto. I had just finished the three day satsang event with Guru Maharaji. I was feeling high and blessed.

I was standing outside the event when I noticed a perfectly proportioned, vertically challenged being with unusual hair and a handsome face. I said that, to me, he looked like a king from some elven kingdom, he said he was. He invited me to come and meet a friend of his who he said had unusual capabilities.

I was up for it so got on a bus and arrived at a suburban house, we went in and there was someone playing the piano the same phrase over and over. Each time the man beside him told him in no uncertain terms he had to do it again and again. It seemed like the piano player was literally frying, some kind of strange transformation was going on for him.

The elf king introduced me to a man called Joey who looked a bit like a Raphelite angel with curly blond hair and a beautiful face. I sat down meditating until he was done with the other guy. Then he came over and sat in an office chair by a desk. I was sitting in the full lotus enjoying the focus that remained after 3 days of satsang. He asked me if I thought I was focused, given that I was in the full lotus and locked in I nodded yes.

Suddenly he clapped his hands once, loudly and all my energy disassembled and my presence seemed to be beyond my body. Then he lent forward and turned into my father, I don't mean he looked a bit like my father I mean he completely changed into my dad and then used a name that only my dad ever called me! I was flabbergasted to say the least. Then he sat back and started to speak like a Mahatma I had just listened to at the event, Charanand. Not only speaking like him but he transformed into him wearing Indian clothes of a mahatma and his face was exactly like the mahatmas!

Now I was really shocked and not quite so sure of myself. Then he started laughing and transformed before my very eyes into the Fool from the Tarot covered in shiny pearl like sequins, he sparkled in his transcendent glory laughing at my reaction to his display.

After that I tried to maintain some composure and offer a little conversation but I was just too gone. This man Joey was a real shape shifter. Apparently, with people who were very entrenched in their ego identity, he would take the form of a tiger and roar at them!

I never saw anyone like him before or since and I still don't really understand what happened I had taken no drugs or done anything to merit this kind of phenomena. But I left with the feeling that I was not quite as great as I thought I was!

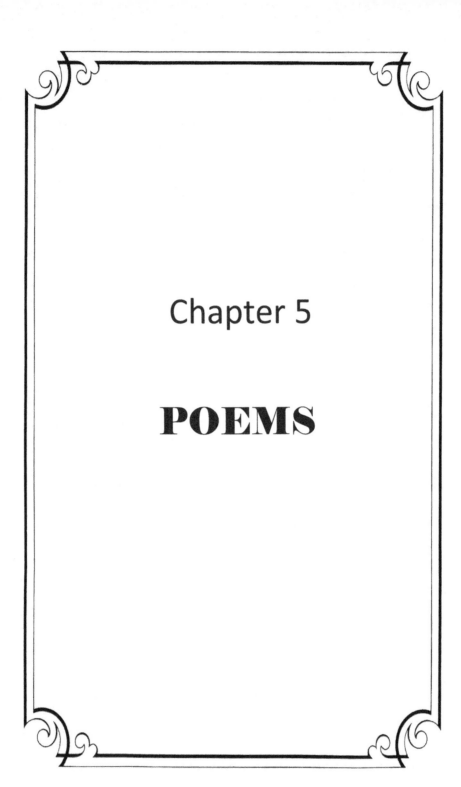

Chapter 5

POEMS

BIRTHING COMPASSION

Accept and lovingly, with tenderness, embrace the fact that your main concern is looking good to yourself and others. Accept and lovingly embrace the fact that you don't actually care that much about others unless it benefits you. Accept and tenderly embrace, allowing plenty of space for the fact that you are sometimes arrogant and mean spirited.

Accept and tenderly embrace the fact that you are angry, very angry about many things,

Accept and tenderly embrace with compassion all the darkness, unresolved stuff, all that's hidden everything that conflicts with your enlightened idea of who you are, embrace it, give it room to be, allow it to appear, let it be.

Accept and tenderly embrace whoever you find yourself to be don't run away into the absolute, saying it's not real when for you it really is.

Accept and lovingly embrace with kindness the wounded one who got hurt, whose dreams did not come true, that one who is unloveable and unwanted, the broken one, accept and lovingly embrace without judgement that one.

Accept allow, admit and open up to the looser, the addict, that bitter one, the hater and the all knowing one,

Accept, bring forth, embrace tenderly your loneliness and self imposed isolation allow it to be released.

Accept tenderly and warmly embrace the secret shame and guilt that you have heaped upon yourself, allow it to be present.

Accept and lovingly embrace the fact that you are not who you thought you were and that life is not what you thought it would be, allow disappointment to be, accept your grief with tenderness.

Now look at the one who has been feeling the miracle of acceptance of what actually is without judgement.Compassion is born, offer it to others.

PROSTRATE

Prostrate yourself to the mountains they are taller than you

Prostrate yourself to the ocean it is deeper than you

Prostrate yourself to the sky it is vaster than you

Prostrate yourself to the river is more flowing than you

Prostrate yourself to the wind it is more free than you

Prostrate yourself to the child it is more innocent than you

Prostrate yourself to the earth and find your place again

Prostrate to Love and restore your heart

Prostrate to intelligence you are not so smart.

Prostrate to kindness maybe it comes your way.

Prostrate yourself whilst feeling remorse.

Prostrate in reverence to the Supreme and Sacred.

Prostrate to the past for having you in it,

Prostrate to the future that all might be well

Prostrate in the present it's the only place you can.

Prostrate to your mother for giving your life,

Prostrate to your father for the gift of his seed.

Prostrate to the beggar and his sovereign heart.

Prostrate to the enlightened and ask for help.

Prostrate in your heart find some humility.

Prostrate to those beings greater than you

Prostrate to life and admit defeat.

Prostrate to your beloved so they may appear as divine.

Prostrate to arise on the Noble Path.

Prostrate as a way of putting your burden down.

Prostrate to gain merit to share.

Prostrate in deep gratitude for all that is.

Prostrate to acknowledge the mistakes you have made.

Prostrate and humbly ask for help

Prostrate to the gods for their special help,

Prostrate to gain access to the mystery of gnosis and cognition.

Prostrate to the goddess that she might answer your call.

Prostrate in the knowing that everything passes.

Prostrate into the profound truth of no self.

Prostrate yourself relinquish your ego

Prostrate once and make it last forever

THE WAY TO LOVE

Under all circumstances Reality, this radiant awareness, is unchanging.

Every moment is dependant upon it and powered by it. The surrender is into that Awareness.

The perceiver, the perceiving and the perceived,

Which are just designations,

All floating in a field of permeating suchness.

When consciousness touches upon Awareness, immediate awakening.

It is possible to completely dissolve into this Awareness,The very source of Love.

Awareness is unassailable, nothing can change it or be apart from it.

There are treasures in the Heart that are discovered one after the other

Jewelled imprints of those who arose before

Marking an invisible pathway to ultimate Reality.

Once there is Knowing, Knowledge is not quite so

exciting.

All Knowledge is but a few drops out of the ocean of Knowing.

When the mental consciousness touches awareness there is

Omniscient knowingness within which insights and revelations spark.

When the consciousness of the sense of touch is lifted to Awareness

One sees the body as a bunch of sensations without solidity.

And the final body is boundless.

Everything is enlightened upon arising.

How is it as experience

That Awareness does not come or go?

Everywhere equally always present, it is the true luminosity.

All other lights have cause and consequence in the play.

The last thing before duality ends?

The perceiver sees it Self.

Behind everything, the miraculous substratum of life.

Any moment that your consciousness is lifted to It

You will start enlightening.

The aim and end of all paths.

There is the blissful fire of pure knowing.

The answer comes by grace as direct seeing.

Happening quicker and quicker for more and more

The Awakening of Humanity

Powered by our every conscious moment.

And what of love?

Love is the divine intention suchness is love

No reason, no lover, no act of loving

Love is the supreme reality

Utterly unthinkable.

Love is causeless ecstatic presence

More than everything put together is love.

THE VANISHING

No past infringing,

No old emotions waiting to be felt.

No hopes for future.Nothing to regret,

No wounded child waiting to be loved

No trauma to unwind,

No accumulation to gather,

Nothing to find, no more searching.

No idea that could make a difference,

Nothing to learn or perfect.

Nothing to hold on to,No one to hold.

No one to pray to.

No state to develop.

Nothing to avoid or cling to.

No view encompasses it,

No point of view.

Nobody waiting or hoping for change

No path or destination.

No awakening or dream.

Nothing encompasses it.

Seeing without looking,

Thoughts arise without a thinker.

Dancing molecules before the vanishing

Beyond mind and matter.

You will never know.

LIGHTEN UP!

You are never going to fix it so put it down!

Stop becoming start being,

The first step is the hardest,

Remember people are always talking about themselves even when the subject is you,

The real you is untouched by all that's happened.

Being kind makes you a nice person!

Take off your ego and put on your crown.

No one got enlightened by being moderate.

Sometimes a good choice is all it takes.

Give up that things have to change before you can be happy. It's possible to be happy standing in shit.

You are loveable exactly as you are.

If you had the same causes and conditions as them you would be exactly the same

"Once there was a way to get back home."(the Beatles) look it might still be here....

Sacrifice being special for being unique,

Turn the other cheek unless a good slap is in order.

Never give up unless you are being stubborn.

What makes the impossible possible is Grace

You never know when it's going to show up and save the day!

If you can watch your breath without interfering that's really good.

If you want great relationship be interested rather than interesting.

Mostly your thoughts arise from your mood and not reality. Don't believe their hype.

If you look within you won't find anyone, this can be initially alarming but you will get over it.

This world is empty and meaningless, being fulfilled you invent the meaning.

A lot of people realise the truth after death which is a pity but better than nothing.

When love calls come running.

However smart you become you will always need a Master

If you don't take acton to save the planet you will be cursed from the future.

THE ULTIMATE MEDITATION

Sit with eyes closed

Do nothing.

Don't use any techniques,

Don't focus on any thing.

Don't visualise or try to create a state,

Don't try and achieve or attain anything.

Don't try and recreate any past experience.

Forget your body,

Forget your life story and the part you are playing,

Forget about the past and the future don't go there.
Don't entertain or suppress any thoughts.

Ignore your commentary.

Don't run from what is uncomfortable,

Don't rush to anything pleasant.

Don't try and ascend or centre or go within

Don't breathe yourself, don't interfere, let it be.

Do nothing just let everything be as it is.

Be with what actually is right now,

Be what actually is right now.

Surrender means do nothing at all,

Let the doer dissolve.

Let it be what it is without interpretation.

A subject looking at an object no more.

XR

The truth of this moment
Is not endless love.

The truth of this moment is not unchanging
Awareness,The truth of this moment is not
unfathomable peace.

That's the absolute forever.

This moment, this time,

In this now

The silent wailing in our hearts

The gnashing of teeth

The palpitations of panic

The mind jamming frequencies

The paranoid projections

The endless sanctioned lies,

The deep denial in our own style

The screaming forests and clogged oceans

The poisonous skies and more lies.

In your voice when you called to arms

I heard a lion roar.

When you made your stand

A giant tree filled your spirit

A forest sprung up right there in the street.

As they carried you off I saw a saint

Speaking so eloquently without a single word.

In that moment the world changed.

And then as another was taken off

The world changed again.

We sat in silence just ahead of an ocean of grief

Whose waves from time to time lapped on our
breaking hearts.

Someone rose and shouted an impassioned plea

"Feel the grief, let all the sorrows arise in you now,

Don't be afraid to feel you must open your heart

And feel to know the truth of where we are."

Then, silently approaching, angels dressed in blood
Carrying the remembrance of the extinct

Ignited deep compassion

And the world changed again.

THE CLEAR LIGHT

The Clear Light

Is not white

or gold

or purple

or electric blue

It's clear.

The clear light

does not radiate

or emanate

or shine.

The clear light

has no opposite

darkness is filled with it.

The clear light

is everywhere equally

and never goes out

or changes

or moves.

The clear light

does not have a source

and casts no shadow.

the clear light

is where everything without exception

arises from and returns to.

The clear light

contains no particles

and makes no beams

has no dimension.

Brilliance and clarity

Sheer luminescence.

the form of emptiness.

The clear light is beyond the beyond and everywhere
else. After the end, before the beginning and all the
way through the clear light.

THE SKY

This sky is clear even when it's foggy,

The sky is pure even in pollution.

Sky is always fresh even though aeons of weather
pass through it.

This sky is the same everywhere

It is never more in one place than another.

The sky embraces everything but remains untouched.
The Sky has infinite centres.

The sky has no source or destination, it never moves.

Only the sky never changes.

The sky sings in the silence and shines in darkness.

When everything vanishes at the end of a dream
Only the sky remains,

Skylike awareness- the clearing for all life.

BAD WEATHER

Don't live in fear of bad weather

Recognise the unchanging sky that you are.

Fear and worry

Have dynamic and creative influence.

Who you are being that it is will give you how you get it, So get your head out of there!

Come to your highest knowing,

Hold yourself there,

This is the best tactic

For getting the best outcome.

That presence,

Silence and stillness are the greatest teacher.

You can get still and then you can get very still,

Then you can be stillness.

There's more, there's always more.

The sky remains the sky no matter what goes on in it, Ferocious storms, exploding bombs,

The sky remains untouched.

Sky-like awareness is who I am.

Chapter 6

108 Questions For Self Enquiry

1. Who am I?

2. Who is me?

3. Who was I before my first thought?

4. Who was I before I was named?

5. Is there a part of me that has never changed?

6. Is there a part of me that does not evolve?

7. Who asks who am I?

8. Who watches that one who asks who am I?

9. How do I know that I am?

10. Who knows I am dreaming when asleep?

11. Who remains in deep dreamless sleep?

12. Who is the source of my thoughts?

13. How do I know I am thinking?

14. What is aware of my thinking yet does not think?

15. What is aware of my emotional responses yet is unaffected by them?

16. Who recognises my confusion yet is not confused?

17. The one who recognises my sadness, is that one sad?

18. What sees even when my eyes are closed?

19. Who hears what I am listening to?

20. Who looks through these eyes?

21. The one who looks through these eyes does it get affected by what it sees?

22. Is there a place where I end?

23. Am I in the body or the body is in me?

24. When I am in deep dreamless sleep where am I?

25. Who perceives me breathing?

26. Am I who I think I am?

27. Who in me knows no sin, shame or guilt?

28. Who listens to me think yet says nothing?

29. Who watches me make mistakes and never judges?

30. Who wants for nothing?

31. Do I have the sense of I AM?

32. Does that mean I am?

33. Who is the one who feels deep Peace and stillness?

34. What about me is real?

35. What in me is uncreated, unborn and boundless?

36. What is more subtle than any imagination?

37. What is more subtle than any thoughts or concepts?

38. What is more subtle than any feeling or emotion?

39. What is more subtle than any state of consciousness?

40. What is more subtle than any realm manifest or unmanifest?

41. What is more subtle than any perception?

42. What is the substratum beneath my persona?

43. Do I have an edge?

44. Is there something in me uncorrupted by time?

45. What is the domain through which my thoughts flow?

46. What is the source of causeless joy in me?

47. If I lost my memory who would I be?

48. When asleep dreaming is everything equally unreal?

49. What watches attention being focused?

50. Am I some body ?

51. From where does my kindness arise?

52. From where does love arise?

53. What is more subtle than space?

54. Is being high nearer to the real?

55. Who is the authentic me?

56. Am I always acting?

57. The one who measures my success and failures is that who I am?

58. The one who evaluates life and everything in it, giving names, is that who I am?

59. Am I the role I play in life, the actor or something else?

60. Whose mind is it?

61. What is it that the mind itself is based on?

62. Is there something in me that cannot be broken, damaged or upset?

63. Is there something about me that the intellect cannot grasp?

64. What is the one source of suffering in me?

65. The one who knows I suffer does it suffer?

66. What is my body when I astrally project?

67. My thoughts of cause and effect are they concept or reality?

68. Is there a part of me for whom nothing ever happens?

69. Is there a part of me that is neither created,

sustained or destroyed?

70. Who is it that I am that feels love?

71. Who the past says I am, is that who I am?

72. Who others say I am, is that who I am?

73. What is the clearing within which everything happens for me?

74. Who my thoughts say I am, is that who I am?

75. Who results show me to be, is that who I am?

76. The feelings, intuitions and realisations I have is that who `I am`?

77. The dreams, hopes and fears that I have is that who I am?

78. Who is the "I" that rises falls, thinks feels and comes in and out of consciousness.?

79. Beyond the sense "I AM" am I?

80. Who senses that "I AM"?

81. Who senses IAM boundless, spacious pure presence?

82. Who am I beyond subject/object paradigm?

83. Who am I when sight, seer and the seen are non different?

84. Who am I when the perceiver and the perceiving and the perceived are collapsed?

85. Who am I when absolutely no difference is seen just like in a dream?

86. Who am I when everything is seen as empty and meaningless?

87. Who am I when there is no centre, no body and no breath?

88. Who am I when peace is ..but not felt.

89. Who am I when there is just beginingless, unsurpassed, causeless joy?

90. Who am I when all that exists is unreal yet I am it all?

91. What is meaning, the meaning that I AM?

92. Who am I that underlies all that is?

93. Who am I that can never be seen?

94. Who am I that everything reflects?

95. Who am I that has never moved yet every movement is within me?

96. Who am I that everything has its existence then disappears leaving me untouched?

97. Who am I when I am equally distributed everywhere?

98. Who am I when undivided, supreme and imperishable?

99. Who am I when I embrace all things, states and beings in unbounded love?

100. Who am I when I am both the drop in the ocean and the ocean in a drop?

101. Who am I that knows my self through you?

102. Who am I that knows nothing ever is, was or could be apart from me?

103. Beyond all forms, thoughts and states of consciousness is what?

104. In every single moment of life, unchanging is what?

105. Above, beyond, within and throughout is what?

106. Who do all gods prostrate to?

107. What is the Supreme Shiva's secret?

108. Who is what they are looking for?

Who I am not:

1. What holds us back from the Presence of Self is misidentification:

2. my body nor the 4 subtle bodies

3. the thinker of my spontaneously arising thought

4. the sense of myself

5. the ego or persona with its traits and characteristics

6. who the past says I am

7. what I have done or do

8. what I have achieved

9. what I possess

10. what I think

11. my opinions

12. my emotions

13. that which could die or be born

14. the 5 different kinds of breath

15. changed by the passing of time

16. changed by any events that happen

17. who people say I am

18. who I think I am

19. my point of view

20. my realisation and understandings

21. my memories

22. the dreamer or my dreams

23. found within the body/mind

24. the atman light particle or soul

25. my past or future lives

26. my talents and abilities

27. the sum total of all my experience

28. my name

29. me

30. separate from all that is

31. in the domain of mind or matter

32. anything perceivable

33. the intellect or the capacity for logic and reason

34. the product of a genetic line

35. what is signified by "I"

36. bound by time or space

37. any size

38. any form

39. any dimension

40. objectifiable or reify-able

41. imaginable or visualisable

42. God or any deity

43. an idea

44. unreal

45. finite

46. that which desires

47. what is seen in a mirror

48. my states of consciousness

49. that which moves

50. anything that can be found

51. ever not there

Chapter 7

Guided Meditation

You can have your eyes open in which case look at a fixed point and try not to blink try not to blink and just keep open and or you can close your eyes okay so first let's be clear that you are eligible you are invited

you are called

The way is clear for you, you have come for this, the time is

now, it's you,

you sovereign being, you holy soul,

you immaculate creation.

The call comes from your knowing,

The call comes from your heart,

The call comes from the future,

The call comes from the present,

The call comes from the angels

The call comes from life

The call comes from all you know.

So first let us become aware of the environment that we're I in whether there be noises, smells, temperature and recognise that we're in an environment but we're not actually interested in anything about it.

Just let everything in the environment be,

Don't make any wishes that it would be different

Just accept the environment you find yourself in right now and let it be.

You might even mentally say "I accept where I am".

Then moving into the body

bring your attention to the top of your head,

feel what you're feeling on the top of your head,

is there any energy, any movement, any sensation at all?

Now bring your attention to your forehead,

around the sides of your head coming down.

To your eyeballs and their sockets,

to your ears

to your jaw,

to your neck

to your shoulders can you feel your clothes on your

shoulders are they tense are they relaxed?

Coming down your arms, elbows.

Feeling your hands what does it feel like having hands?

Are they cold or tingling or are they pulsing?

Now come down your front from your chest,your tummy,

your stomach and to the ground.

And your back coming down your spine to your pelvis

And the ground.

Feel your weight feel your weight and your thighs

to your knees, your calves,

to your feet, to your toes.

The sensations of having a physical body.

Being present to them, we're not interested in them, there they are let them be don't wish them another way just accept as it is don't try and change the circumstance of your body.

Now bring yourself in to your emotional body

choose to feel what you're feeling,

to feel what you're feeling,

momentums of feeling

different streams of feeling coming out of the past:

Perhaps you've been feeling anxious

perhaps you've been feeling grief at the way things are

going generally

or grief of things that have happened in your own life,

perhaps you've been feeling helpless,

perhaps you've been feeling hopeless.,

perhaps you've been feeling excited

perhaps you've been feeling tremendous

love perhaps you are sensing what's going on.

Where are those feelings? Allow them.

Anything that you've been holding back and suppressing

Now accept and feel.

Allow it to be,

don't get carried away by it

you're just observing it

you're noticing what you're feeling,

but you're not interested,

you're going somewhere else.

And there's your thoughts,

your mental thoughts happening in your mental body, same as they were

not interested.

Your commentary about how you're doing, how I'm doing, not interested this time. Come back later!

Anything that the mind has to say right now,

we're really not interested,

we're going somewhere else.

The part you've been playing in this life,

of a man or a woman or something else,

a parent, a friend, a brother, a sister, a lover

the job you've been doing,

the functions that you perform,

the part you play in this life

supported by states of consciousness, thoughts, feelings and sensations,

all of them release,

none of that, we're not interested.

just put them down.

Now that we're open

Mentally or out loud say the word I-I-I-I keep going and notice what is happening when you do this

it's pulling you out of your mind and pulling you into your heart.

If you're experiencing this you're probably feeling a sense of centring in the heart, keep going I-I-I-I

Keep going,

perhaps a warmth developing,

perhaps an excitement because this works

going deeper and deeper into the I,

the subtle sense 'I am'

everything else aside just 'I am'

keep going I-I-I-I

now you should be feeling peace

and stillness

simplicity

clarity

and freedom.

As you vacate this space,

coming into the heart, there is love.

Opening into a field of love.

Your breath now is much more shallow and it's nature is love

your breath gently fanning your heart

emanating love,

in a field of love.

Will you allow something that fantastic?

So here you sit on the throne in your own heart

the sovereign being of silence,

impartial awake, present loving in a field of love.

This presence is everywhere,

Always. Already.

In this special moment in time

let us offer up

prayers in words and vibrations,

the flame in the core of our heart is lit

we are present to love.

Recognizing that we are here because of our parents, our grandparents our great-grandparents, our great-great- great-grandparents, our great-great-great-great-great grandparents and so on and so on and so on innumerable beings brought us to this point and all of them are interconnected, we call for their blessing and we send our blessing backwards through time

we let them know it will be okay,

we let them know that love is being

victorious in our lives.

We call in our guardian angel,

who hovers just outside of our conscious awareness most of the time,

that comes to us in dreams visions and intuitions,

"thank you, thank you please guide me

please help me, please show me how to maintain my presence

in the field of love

as a lover."

Bring to mind all those people that we feel we're not complete with

and we accept them as they are.

We no longer try to change anybody or make anybody

wrong for being who they are right now.

Forgive everybody for everything.

I forgive everyone for everything.

Stop psychically punishing anyone.

Let everyone be,

so that this love can flow through all parts of your
life all the domains

wherever you have withdrawn your love give it up

let love flow. let love be.

Forgive, release.

Let your life drama be

detach, disassociate, radiate this now.

recognise this

you are whole

you are not wounded

are not broken, you are whole

you are free

you are freedom itself

confirm this

you're full in this emptiness

you are presence in this emptiness

how you think it is, put that down

be brave enough to see how it actually is

and who you actually are.

now we recognize

that although we are unassociated and free

we exist in a unified field with all other beings and
all of life

so let us now choose to emanate consciously love
into the

collective,

The collective consciousness.

radiate love

into the entire matrix of humanity

all of it interconnected nothing separate.

There are beings awakening

to the reality of what truly is and together

may we regenerate heaven on earth

may we respect all life

may there be a great awakening to the wonder of
love

inconceivable love

now

at this conscious choice point

choose love, choose happiness

choose compassion

choose kindness

choose generosity

choose love

commit yourself

to being awake and doing what it takes

choose to be that your liberation is now

recognise that all is

in your mind's eye

you can see the globe of this beautiful earth

and around it an aura of pure white light

pulsing, living, blessing the entire planet

from the very smallest level of subatomic particles

right the way up to the globe itself,

everything blessed

focus and visualise this light pulsing through everything.

it's a good thing that you are here

know that you have everything that you need to be all that you can be

you already have everything that you need to be all that you can be

three Oms

A short story of mystery and intrigue, romance and miracles!

Chapter 8

The Lama In The Whale

"The Dalai Lama can choose to incarnate as an animal or an insect if he wants." His Holiness 14th Dalai Lama.

By
Tim Williams

Chapter 1

The last breath of the 14th Dharma Lama came suddenly, like a bad smell on a hot afternoon, as he was enjoying reading a book about whales. A gasp, are asping gurgle then his final exhalation.

Unceremoniously this great Buddhist master fell forward and the last thing he saw in this life was the smiling eye of a great whale.

Realising what had happened he quickly awakened to the reality of life without his body. He had been training daily for this moment of death for most of his life. As a Tibetan Buddhist monk he had studied and taught the teachings of the Tibetan Book of the Dead, the classic treatise on the process that unfolds at the time of death and thereafter.

As his awareness grew he became conscious of his sensitivity expanding and becoming more acute, he found himself looking down on his body which was bathed in the sunlight of a beautiful Himalayan afternoon. He felt calm and knew he must begin saying prayers to call on the protector deities and his own Lamas to come and help him journey through the Bardos, the phases and stages of integration and resolution of his past life.

As he started with the mantras which were so deeply engrained in his being after so many millions of repetitions, the Lamas appeared in his inner vision in their subtle bodies, radiating kindness, light and a sense of welcome. He felt a great joy and his heart flowed towards them without a second thought. The Dharma Lama felt his subtle body ascending and as he looked up at the end of a long tunnel above him, he saw a beautiful light scintillating and inviting him forward. He knew if he went that far it would mean no future lives for him and his complete emancipation into suchness, completion, the end of the journey, the fulfilment of the Path. Nirvana.

He was just about to move on up to his ultimate destiny when his attention was drawn to the mournful and deeply sorrowful sound of a little girl crying in distress. Her sadness and desperation were unbearable for him. A dilemma arose in him: should he go on up to his own liberation or go and see what was troubling that child? A great love arose in his heart and he chose to go and see what was troubling the child. His mystic vision opened and he saw where exactly the weeping was coming from. What he beheld was a silvery beach lit by moon light with the tide out and there washed up on the sand was the lifeless bodies of twenty-one beleaguered whales and standing beside one was a little girl consumed with grief at the fate of these magnificent creatures. A profound feeling of compassion arose within the Dharma Lama and a vow he had made many times to return and help sentient beings all come to complete universal enlightenment was remembered and activated powerfully in his being.

At that point everything changed and he found himself standing in front of The Buddha Chenrezi in a great jewelled temple filled with liberated and shining beings who seemed to be silently cheering him.

His heart was filled with great astonishment at the glory he beheld. Every day he had prayed to Chenrezi and as the 14th Dharma Lama, the head of his ancient lineage, he was said to embody this very Buddha but now here in the bardo the sight was just so fantastic he felt very small indeed. The Buddha smiled at the Dharma Lama: "so you would return to the world of human kind, the world of suffering and sorrow and renounce your Liberation and the chance to live in this Heavenly reality?" The Dharma Lama looked up into the eyes of the enlightened one for a timeless moment and dropped his gaze. He nodded with deep certainty and love for all beings. He folded his hands together and made a deep bow before this wondrous lord of enlightenment.

As he bowed his head the entire scene vanished and he found himself hurtling through the sky, it was nighttime and there was a ferocious storm with thunder, lightening and driving rain. He looked down and saw a turbulent ocean, huge waves crested and raged beneath him. He was drawn by a powerful force through the sky as if destiny was demanding his immediate attendance in a particular place and at a particular time.

The last thing he saw was a great whale rise up, massive, out of a huge wave before crashing down disappearing into the depths. Then it all went dark and still. For a long time.

The Dharma Lama had not been prepared for this, he had no idea where he was or what was happening. Where was he? What bardo was he in? Was this some hell realm, some place of integration? Was it his own mind?

After a while he began to realise that he was consciousness within a large living being, a very large living being. Then it dawned on him he had transmigrated into the body of a whale. His mental continuum, thoughts, memories, realisations, spiritual knowledge and power had arrived inside the mind of a whale.

Chapter 2

The passing of the 14th Dharma Lama sent ripples around the world. He had lived a very long and virtuous life and was loved by pretty much everyone except of course the Chinese. The Chinese government saw the office of the Dharma Lama and the Great 14th himself as a major obstruction in the fulfilment of their desire to unify China. The Tibetans would not concede that Tibet was ever part of China and stubbornly refused to kowtow to what they saw as the evil empire. This view was horrifically punctuated by the self immolation of over 120 Tibetans.

When the Noble Buddha passed from this life it was said that there were two kinds of reactions that people had. Those who had followed the teachings and done the practice experienced deep meditation and profound peace whilst those who were of a more devotional disposition experienced inconsolable grief. So it was with the Dharma Lama, some dedicated monks went into deep states of realisation and reported feeling the transmission of a great dispensation whilst most others were very upset and there was much wailing and gnashing of teeth in the Tibetan community but also around the world.

After sometime it was decided that he would be cremated in a huge open space in Dharmsala where he had lived, in the foothills of the Himalayas, since his heroic arrival from India many decades ago.

People started gathering immediately, the announcement was made and in the two weeks prior to the ceremony over a million people descended on the small town.

As the day approached dignitaries and other not able from around the world arrived and then just before the ceremony world leaders arrived in private jets to pay their last respects to this remarkable being.

On the day before it rained, in fact it poured, but the half million Tibetan and others from the Himalayan region who had already taken their places refused to budge. It became a deluge and the site turned to mud and the weather seemed to add to the general despondency felt by the collective.

On the morning of the cremation the rain stopped and there was a great bustle getting every one seated. Then the great horns started blowing, the crash of cymbals and the sound of high pitched trumpets announced the arrival of the His Holiness the Dalai Lama and many High Lamas who brought with them the Dharma Lamas body which was to be placed on top of a pile of sacred wood from Assam. Chosen because for some reason burning bodies do not smell when this particular wood is used.

A great silence fell over the huge crowd, monks could be heard chanting the auspicious prayers directing the departed on his onward journey.

As the great fire was lit and the first flames were seen a murmuring went through the crowd with some folk pointing up into the sky and slowly and surely a rainbow took shape and became clear as great beams of sunshine blessed the sodden crowd. There was a feeling of wonder and comfort at this auspicious sight which continued to grow until a second rainbow also appeared vivid against the mountain backdrop. People cheered and there were tears of joy.

Several months after the final ritual all the High Lama's were called together to set about finding the next incarnation, the 15th Dharma Lama. It was decided that this should happen quickly because if there was too much delay the Chinese government would choose a candidate of their own, someone who they could control.

Monks were sent out far and wide to Tibet and across the Himalayan region in search of a young boy who would be the next Dharma Lama. Once found he would be bought to Dharmsala where possessions of the previous Dharma Lama, his rosary, a bowl he used, his glasses, and other items would be mixed with similar objects not belonging to His Holiness, if the child was the true reincarnation then he should be able to choose the items that were his in his previous life and leave those that were not.

The 14th Dharma Lama had a strange and long relationship with an old woman called Choden Guten. She was a medium, an oracle and channeled wrathful deities and protector spirits. These beings would occupy her body and give messages about the fate of Tibet and the Dharma Lama.

When the Chinese invaded Tibet it was Choden Guten that was responsible for awakening the Dharma Lama in the middle of the night and helping him escape over the mountains just in time before the Chinese authorities arrived to arrest him. She had been told by the spirits exactly what to do. For this reason the Dharma Lama always kept her close and made her the State, and his personal, Oracle. The problem was however that channeling these ferocious wrathful deities had its toll on Choden Guten and to keep herself pacified she had taken to drinking alcohol and so was often very outspoken.

Most times she had to be held up until the spirit entered her at which time she would whirl about laughing and shouting at all and sundry. In that state she could see everyone exactly as they were and would tell them or simply look at them and laugh hysterically.

It was decided that Dorje Lama who was the aide to the Dharma Lama for many years, should go and ask Choden Guten if she would help find the next incarnation. He really did not want to do this because she was so unpredictable and fierce but he knew that he must because she was probably their best chance of finding the next Dharma Lama.

Choden Guten lived in a small house given to her by the Dharma Lama and it was surrounded by a high stone wall. Between the wall and the house was a garden within which were two prowling tibetan mastiffs. To get to the door Dorje Lama had to pass by these ferocious guardians. He had a brainwave and on the way to see her and stopped off at a butcher shop and bought two pieces of meat. When he got to the house he unwrapped them and tossed them over the wall and quickly made his way across the garden to the front door and knocked loudly. No reply, the dogs looked up, he banged again. This time he heard some cursing and crashing about inside.

The dogs slowly wandered over growling menacingly showing their fangs and curling their lips. The door opened Dorje Lama rushed in and slammed the door. "What do you want you lily livered one?' the oracle chortled,

"O Choden Guten only you can help us we must find the next Dharma Lama before the Chinese government seize the initiative!"

He looked at her and saw she was very intoxicated and unsteady on her feet. She seemed to be looking at a point above his head.

Her place was a complete mess, old bottles were strewn across the floor, cans of dog food, old newspapers and general chaos.

She caught him looking disdainfully making a judgement about her,

"You are nothing, you know nothing and everything about you is fake, fake monk, fake, monkey ahah"' she roared at him. Dorje felt his heart palpitating, "yes Choden what you say is true, I am just pretending what to do?"

"What to do? haha"? she laughed and laughed collapsing into a chair.

She went quiet and completely still except for her eyes which seemed to be moving intensely under her lids.

Dorje sat at her feet and waited looking at her extraordinary face which was lined and ravaged by time but there was also a hidden beauty and innocence. He confessed to himself he had never seen a face quite like it.

He sat there for over an hour then she seemed to be snoring. He wondered what to do, should he wake her and risk her wrath at being brought back from a communion with the spirit world or should he just leave but then he would have to face the mastiffs in the garden. He decided to wait.

He wondered how such a crazy one could really help, then a picture of the Dharma Lama on her alter seemed to wink at him and he remembered that she had once saved his life and the fate of Tibet.

At that moment Choden Guten, High Oracle to His Holiness the 14th Dharma Lama sat up and belches heroically, her foul breath reached Dorje Lama who knew better than to react.

She started mumbling mantras as she tapped a circular silver disc garnished with semi precious jewels that hung as a necklace over her heart. Her eyes closed rolled up inside her head and then she seemed to be talking to someone in the invisible realms.

At which point she started laughing and laughing hysterically, so much so she fell off her seat onto the floor still laughing, she cried out,

"It's all very fishy, very fishy!' and burst into more guffaws of laughter. Rinpoche tried to question her but she would say nothing about what was so funny.

Then he helped her back into her chair and she whispered into his ear "Very important Little Sonam Tulku must go to Kailas to Arya Tara's cave." Then she fell into a deep sleep and he knew the audience with the State Oracle was over.

Chapter 3

Jonny Tibet was the only internationally known star Tibet had ever produced. Now in his late 40's Jonny was living well off the royalties from his 10 albums and 8 movies. He was a Tibetan Buddhist and a friend of the 14th Dharma Lama in so far as one could be.

He got preferential treatment at teachings and functions because he had donated a large amount to build a monastery in southern India.

He had a certain charm to him which made people he met warm to him and perhaps that is why he became such a star. Nowadays he was living a quieter life but back in the day there were screaming fans where ever he went in the Asian region.

Jonny was on a flight to Ballina in Australia, he was headed for Byron Bay where he had heard of a Marine Park-The Oceanarium that was for sale. He had a plan to buy it and turn it into a Marine hotel resort.

Sitting next to him in business class was a rather attractive woman who seemed to be a bit nervous and uptight. Jonny thought, maybe she was not a keen flyer.

She dropped the pen she had been writing with and Jonny reached down to pick it up at the same time as she did their hands touched at the pen, heads bent down they looked at each other there was a definite moment, a frisson between them.

Jonny had got there first so handed her the pen. " I am Jonny Tibet who are you?" he flashed his famous grin.

"My name is Geraldine" she replied somewhat underwhelmed.

Jonny liked her even though he felt that she would be a challenging person to talk with. They started chatting and it turned out that she had never heard of him and that she was a marine Biologist studying whales and particularly why they kept washing up on beaches apparently having lost there way.

"I have often wondered about that, it's so sad,

why do they do that?"

"We don't really know I am researching for NASA the theory that it may be influenced by astronomical events. Many cetaceans use the Earth's magnetic field to navigate, and their internal compasses could be vulnerable to magnetic anomalies, of the kind caused by solar storms."

She paused but he seemed interested so she continued," The sun occasionally lashes out with streams of charged particles and radiation; perhaps they're also responsible for disorienting whales sending them into dangerous waters. It seems like a far-fetched possibility but one that I am researching."

"It does sound a bit unlikely because there have always been solar storms one would think that nature would have adapted to this and it seems that there are more and more of these strandings?" replied Jonny.

"Well there are more its true and another theory is Cetaceans can be disoriented by the underwater din of human activity, from naval sonar to the seismic airguns used in oil and gas exploration. Several stranding events have been tied to military exercises as well."

"That sounds more likely to me, well good luck with your research it sounds fascinating".

They rested in a companionable silence for a while. "Where are you going?" asked Geraldine

"I am going to look at an old Oceanarium that is up for sale near Byron Bay" he replied.

"Really? You going to fill it with whales and dolphins?"

"Yes and build a hotel complex and a small theme park, there is nothing like that in the area." Replied Jonny proudly.

"They really don't like that you know" Geraldine said tentatively

"Who doesn't like what?"

"Whales don't like being in captivity!" "How do you know that?" challenged Jonny

"Well apart from it being obvious by observation of their behaviours there is one thing that is undeniable the fin on their back goes floppy because they are designed to swim long distances and when they don't this fin collapses." She said with a slight note of disdain in her voice.

"I have to admit I had not thought about

whether they enjoyed it or not, they always look like they are having fun." Jonny realised how naive he sounded but it was true it had not occurred to him.

The moment was broken by a buzzing on Geraldine's phone that was charging on the small table between them. Picking it up she saw a text had arrived from her boss.

"Large Orca whale washed up in storm at Oceanarium north of Byron Bay still alive but not moving suggest you go there asap"

"Which beach is that?" she texted back.

"It's not on the beach it's in the Oceanarium beside the beach washed there by a surge tide during last nights strom.

"Should be there in a couple of hours."

Putting the phone down Geraldine turned to Jonny "you are not going to believe this!"

"What's happened?"

"A large Orca whale has been washed up into the Oceanarium north of Byron Bay! Isn't that where you are going?"

"Yes it is and the Oceanarium is right on the beach, how strange is that?'

"The whale is apparently alive but motionless in the main tank, I am going to see what I can do for it." 'Ok well let's get a ride there together, it seems like the forces of synchronicity are at play!"

"Sure let's do that but what's synchronicity?" she inquired.

"It's like coincidence but more so! when you meet a friend by chance it's a coincidence but when you meet a friend by chance and that meeting has meaning or purpose then it's synchronicity. It's the Universe putting elements where they have to be to fulfil some higher purpose" he replied confidently.

"Are you a Buddhist most Tibetans are I would imagine?"

"Yes I am or at least try to be." he said trying to summon some modesty.

"I was so sorry to hear of the passing of the Dharma Lama. I am not a Buddhist and not sure I even believe in a higher purpose but I was really sad when I heard he had died. In this world a good hearted man is hard to find and whatever else he might have been he was certainly that. Did you ever meet him?" "what I did many times, he was my greatest teacher, his passing was very sad for me because I really loved him." A wave of emotion arose in Jonny tearing his eyes, he looked away quickly but Geraldine had seen and spontaneously placed her hand on his offering comfort.

The stewardess came by Geraldine withdrew her hand and the moment passed.

She stared out of the window thinking about how unlike it was for her to do that and how much she liked him for reasons she could not quite put her finger on.

As business class passengers they were off the plane first and into the limousine that was waiting for Jonny. It was a half hour journey to the Oceanarium.They sat silently each thinking about the other and the strange events that had brought them together.

On arrival they were met by the estate agent a greasy looking man in a sharp suit despite the heat. Before there could be any sales pitch Jonny said:

"This is Miss Geraldine..er " and realised that he did not know her second name.

"Doctor Geraldine Rilet marine biologist here to see to the welfare of the Orca whale?"

"Of course madam come right this way."

They made there way through the complex of small shops, entry hall and then there was the underground viewing area with a huge glass window that allowed viewers to see the whales close up and underwater. They went up the stairs into the arena with it's amphitheatre of seats surrounding a large pool.

There in the centre of the pool completely still was a large black and white Orca whale about 30 feet long. They both stood there looking at the whale somehow astonished at it's stillness. All around the area were bits of wood and other debris from the storm.

"He is in a state of shock, that's why he is so still he may even be concussed but I have to say I have never seen or heard of anything like this before." "How can you tell it's a he?"

"The main difference between a male and a female Orca is the dorsal fins. Males usually have at all straight dorsal fin which can reach up to 6ft in length. Female dorsals are usually a lot smaller and more curved. See how big his fin is?"

Jonny's phone rang he excused himself and walked away

"Dorje how great to hear from you how is it going with the search for the Dharma Lama?

It's what, in Wales? You have found someone in Wales? I can't hear you properly speak slowly!

What? it is a whale what? The 15th Dharma Lama is a whale? Who says this?

What? that old bird she is bat shit crazy! You are sending Sonam Tulku and Rinpoche to Mount Kailas to get confirmation? OK yes of course time is of the essence I will arrange my jet to pick them up from Dharmsala tomorrow to fly to Lhasa and there I will rent a helicopter to fly them to the Mountain. No problem. But Dorje I have a whale here in the Oceanarium I am thinking of buying, buy it? Ok if you say so. Talk soon. jemmy jay jong "

By the end of that afternoon Jonny had taken ownership of the run down Oceanarium and a major cleanup was in operation. He has also arranged for his jet to fly the two monks to Lhasa and a helicopter meet them and take them to Mount Kailas. Things were moving very fast.

Chapter 4

In Dharmsala Dorje Lama, the 14th Dharma Lama's lifelong aide, had been given the job of heading up the team to find the next incarnation of the Dharma Lama. As such he was waiting to see a representative of the Chinese government. A Mr.Chang Yang had been most insistent on being seen. At exactly 11am the delegation arrived at the temple complex and were shown to the reception room reserved for dignitaries.

Dorje came in with some senior monks, the atmosphere was tense.

"Welcome, welcome can we offer you some tea gentlemen?" enquired Lama Dorje.

"We are not here to drink tea, we have come because we feel it is now the responsibility of the Chinese Government to find the next Dharma Lama and so in Tibet we have been looking and we feel we have found an excellent candidate from Kam. He will be here tomorrow and we demand that the Test to establish his authenticity take place as soon as possible." barked Yang.

"Well for the last fourteen incarnations the job of finding the next Dharma Lama has fallen on the senior monks, it's part of a very old tradition, there are strict rules and protocols. However I am sure we can accommodate your wishes." He knew only too well that to upset the Chinese was to create problems for the Tibetans in Tibet.

It was arranged that the first Test should happen the following day which in fact suited Dorje Lama as many people were getting impatient.

The following morning the objects were laid out on a large low table. One of the bowls was the previous Dharma Lama's and four were not, one of the mala beads were his and four were not and also one pair of glasses were his but four were not. Traditionally the candidate had to pick all four items that were his in his last life. If he did so then he would be considered to be the bonafide reincarnation.

A little boy of about 3 years old was brought in by one of the Chinese deligation, he was wearing Tibetan clothes and seemed quite confident. He marched up to the table and was immediately drawn to a mala and picked it up. There was a stir amongst the senior monks who knew that the little child had indeed picked up the mala that belonged to the Dharma Lama. Then the child leaned over and picked up a bowl and a pair of glasses which he gave to Mr. Yang.

Dorje Lama received the objects and turned them over to see if the Dharma Lamas mark was on the bottom or not. The Mala was the Dharma Lamas' but the other two objects were not Mr. Yang was not happy, he accused the monks of adding the marks after.

"Perhaps you would like to see these photos Mr.Yang which show His Holiness with the objects so there can be no doubt". With that the Chinese delegation left with the little boy, who was now not to be the next Dharma Lama, in tow. Later they were to spin it that the little boy had correctly picked an object as if that was all that was required but as no confirmation was forth coming from the Office of the Dharma Lama that story gained no traction but allowed them to return to China without loosing too much face.

Later that day Dorje Lama summoned Sonam Tulku and his aide Rinpoche to his office for a final briefing before they left for Mount Kailas. Sonam Tulku was an authentic reincarnation of another Lama and he had passed the test. He was ten years old with the wisdom and emotional intelligence of an adult.

Everyone loved him because he had such a sunny disposition and an engaging smile added to that he actually looked like a Buddha. Rinpoche, his aide, was of a different mettle. He was in his thirties, a clever man with a pox marked face and unfathomable eyes, who had been serving Sonam Tulku since he was three years old.

"Everything is arranged. You will fly to direct to Ngari Airport this afternoon on arrival you will be transferred to a helicopter after clearing customs and immigration. As you both have Chinese passports this should not be a problem it's a small airport. You will then proceed to Mt. Kailas where you will go to the cave of Arya Tara. Choden Guten, the state Oracle, tells us that you will find some important information as to the next Dharma Lama and that it must be you, Sonam Tulku, who goes and does this. When you find something contact me immediately and no one else. May the great protectors guard and guide you!"

Sonam Tulku looked at Rinpoche and shone a smile which was not returned by Rinpoche who had a sly look on his face, his mind elsewhere.

Everything unfolded like clockwork, the two monks arrived in Ngari, Tibet which is about 250 km from Mt Kailas in Jonny Tibet's private Gulf stream 2 jet, they were cleared through customs with a minimum of formality and were shown to the waiting helicopter. Climbing aboard Sonam Tulku saw two men, a pilot and another unusual looking man sitting next to him. The Tulku immediately knew that this second man was not a co-pilot but a spy. Saying nothing he flashed his winning smile and disarmed the spy who immediately turned away and looked out of the window. Rinpoche nodded subtly to the man as he climbed aboard something that Tulku saw out of the corner of his eye. His intuition was beginning to understand what was happening and he smelt betrayal.

Sonam Tulku had never flown in a helicopter before and was finding it nerve racking but also very exciting he felt he was on a great adventure doing important work which he was. Seeing the approaching mountains from the helicopter was breathtaking and then there was the great Mount Kailas, the most sacred point of pilgrimage to both Hindus and Buddhists. He had heard so much about it, now as it came directly into view he found himself muttering prayers baffled by its glory. The helicopter landed not far from the vast blue lake Manasarovar.

"It's 2pm now we leave 6pm latest you have 4 hours."

The two monks walked off towards the great mountain down the well worn path of the Kora, a sacred walk around the mountain 55 gruelling kilometers long. It was claimed to do this generated very good karma and many Tibetans and others came to this some more than just once and some even did the 55km by making a full prostration then getting up taking a pace and prostrating again.

Rinpoche knew the mountain as he had come before and also he knew where Arya Tara's cave was. They set off and Rinpoche was silent out in front of Sonam Tulku who knew why but had decided to say nothing till the time was right. After an hour or so they rounded a corner and there before them was the entrance to a cave strewn with colourful prayer flags left by pilgrims of the past. Sonam Tulku turned round and saw in the distance the Chinese spy was following them.

They entered into the cave and found it to be really quite large and more like a small temple. There were beautiful paintings of gods, buddhas and bodhisattvas on the walls and in the centre a huge statue of Arya Tara patron goddess of Tibet, sitting one foot down as it was said she was always ready to help. There was a butter lamp lit so they lit several more illuminating the mystical murals.

Sonam Tulku prostrated in front of Tara and

chanted her mantra OM TARE TUTARE TURE SVAHA over and over hoping to attract her attention and gain her blessings because the truth was he had no idea what he was doing here.

At that moment there came a deep rumbling and a rushing sound as rocks rubble and shingle slid down the mountain side blocking the entrance to the cave with them inside it.

Dust was everywhere as it settled it became clear to the two monks that the door way was completely blocked. Tulku sat down closed his eyes calmly. "You're meditating now, here in the middle of a catastrophe?!" shouted Rinpoche hysterically clawing at the rubble.

"Stop that and be calm for a minute, I am trying to remember something."

Rinpoche sat down despondent, head in his hands. After some time Sonam Tulku opened his eyes and declared' "I lived here for some time in a previous life and that entrance we came in was not there then. Behind Tara there should be a passage to another room which has it's own exit further down! Come let's see if I am right, bring a light!"

They eased their way behind the great statue and there was a small passage way that lead into another room. As their butter lamps flickered and lit up the wall they saw it was covered in highly elaborate murals depicting a succession of Dharma Lamas.

"Bring the light here Rinpoche look there is the 13th who was very small and there is the 14th with crowds and what is that? can you see?" he asked amazed by what he thought he saw.

"Looks like a fish where the 15th Dharma Lama should be." his voice trailing off in amazement. "That's not a fish that is a killer whale an Orca see its black and white markings it's a whale! "With great excitement and wonder he pulled out his mobile phone and immediately took several photos.

Just as he did that the plaster, disturbed by the landslide after hundreds of years came off the cave wall and crumbled onto the floor lost forever.

They both jumped aside shocked by one thing happening after another. As the dust settled Sonam Tulku took the butter lamp from Rinpoche who was busy lighting others he had found and walked to where the wall painting had been. To his amazement there was a hole which the plaster painting had covered he put his hand in the hole and felt a wooden box he pulled it out and set it down on the floor.

"Rinpoche look at this it's a terma!"

Termas were buried hidden dharma treasure sometimes actual treasure, buddhas, jewels and such like and sometimes treasures of teachings. The Tibetan Book of the Dead was found buried in 1950 after having been written and buried 500 years earlier by a great Tibetan mystic Padmasambhava it contained the secret teachings about the process of dying and rebirth. "Be careful it looks very old and might crumble if you open it" warned Rinpoche.

Just as he said that an edge crumbled in Sonam Tulkus hand. He carefully wrapped the box with his shawl and placed it in his bag.

"We've got to get out of here now, where's the door?" "It should be down over there" replied the Tulku.

They found where it used to be but it would not budge even though Rinpoche was throwing his whole weight against it.

"Maybe this might help!!" said Sonam Tulku as he bashed the bolt unseen by Rinpoche with a rock and the door flew open to reveal the astonishing brightness of Kailas the sacred mountain.

"We must go and find the Chinese spy he was

following us he may have been swallowed up in the landslide." said Tulku

"What Chinese spy?" replied Rinpoche

"Rinpoche I know you informed the Chinese about our mission but the thing I don't know is why. We have been together for many years and you have always served me faithfully why now this betrayal?" Rinpoche was shocked he did not know that Sonam Tulku knew but he was also glad because keeping secrets of betrayal from him was painful.

"O Sonam Tulku yes I did betray you and I am so ashamed and so sorry but I was approached in Dharmsala by that Chinese co-pilot, he showed me a picture of my family in Lhasa and said I had to help him or bad things would happen to them. He knew my nieces name and school, what could I do?" he sounded desperate and true.

"OK now I understand and it's something that I don't want to talk of ever again to anyone."

"Yes Tulku".

They walked back over the landslide and saw how the cave entrance had been completely buried by tons of rubble. After sometime they saw the helicopter take off and figured that the Chinese spy must have made it back and reported the two monks buried alive in the cave.

They walked on until they returned to where the helicopter had been where, as luck would have it, were a group of Tibetan pilgrims with two 4x4's which happened to have room for them and were indeed heading back to the airport at Ngari some 250 km away.

"O Tulku please sit in the front, here have some tea, are you hungry? We are so happy to help you what wonderful fortune!" Sonam Tulku gave one of his wonderful smiles and replied "it is said that your good karma takes you to Mt. Kailas and your bad karma brings you back. Well it looks like we don't have any hahaha!!" Everyone laughed as they pulled away. The sun was setting over the mighty mountain and turning the Lake from turquoise to gold. After sometime Sonar Tulku had a signal on his phone so sent the photos of the whale and a message to Lama Dorje.

"We found it in Tara's cave there is no doubt it has been long prophesied that the 15th Dharma Lama will be a whale plus a Terma that needs translating will be back midday tomorrow."

Chapter 5

The following day they arrived back in Dharmsala and went straight to see Dorje Lama with the Terma. Sonam Tulku was beaming with delight, this was how things were meant to be he thought.

"So well done you two let's see what you found." Sonam Tulku brought out the box which had beautiful carving of Yamantaka a wrathful protector deity carved on the front. Opening it there were several long oblong parchments lying one on top go the other. The first page apart from some writing which was not legible had an image of two buddhas with a whale in between them simply drawn. Dorje Lama looked quite astonished:"This is very old I would think maybe 300 years or more, we must be careful not to damage it. I have called for the Office of Antiquities to come and examine the parchments and translate to us what they say."

Just then a monk came in seeking the Lamas attention "Its Jonny Tibet on your phone will you take the call" "Jonny yes they have returned from Kailas and the they found a Terma and photos of a tangka painting on the wall of the cave which confirms that the 15th Dharma Lama will be embodied in a black and white whale!" "That's incredible the whale I have here is black and white, you must come and see it immediately!"

"Yes we will come with the State Oracle can we use your plane?"

"Yes of course, it will be refuelled and ready this evening for eight people."

"Wonderful I will send you the photos Sonam Tulk took of the mural now and the Terma report when we have it but keep it secret until we are sure and ready to let the world know." said Dorje Lama.

That afternoon the Terma was carefully examined and subjected to various tests by the monks from the Office of Antiquities who were sworn to secrecy before they opened very carefully the documents and laid them out on a white back lit table. First they gently brushed off extraneous dust and then photographed the sheathes of parchment from all angles.

The document was written in an old version of

Tibetan which one of the monks was able to translate. He took his time and made notes, checked in two reference books went back to the document, made more notes and finally said:"I think you had better call Dorje Lama.."

By the time Dorje Lama arrived at the Office of Antiquities the monk had organised his thoughts: "These documents are extraordinary there is no doubt of their authenticity to my mind, they are extremely old between 350 and 500 years old I would say. But what is written in them is very unusual. Basically they say in the time of darkness when the Land of Snows is invaded by angry beings who poison the land and destroy the dharma, the very lineage of Dharma Lamas will be threatened. It Say that the 15th Dharma Lama will appear in a foreign land far away where there are no mountains at the bottom of the world.

The 14th Dharma Lama will transmigrate into the body of a great whale whose name is to be Kundun. After forty nine days The 15th Dharma Lama will be embodied in this whale for three years, three months and three days."

The monk was trembling as he read the ancient prophecy that would create a shock wave throughout the buddhist community and probably the world, he went on" more than this it describes his life events saying there will be five miraculous happenings. The first will be his appearance as a whale, the second will be that he will cause great healing to anyone who comes near to him, the third is that he will deliver a teaching and the fourth is in his association with other whales and the fifth will be the manner of his departure."

They all stood stunned in silence for a moment. Lama Dorje broke the silence" say nothing about this to anyone, do you understand say nothing to anyone. If the Chinese find out about this they will try and stop it absolute secrecy is essential."

Jonny received the photos and the report on the Terma and had to sit down it was just so fantastic but thinking about it he could see there was a massive synchronicity basically and he wanted to play his part to the full.

He called Geraldine who was working on samples she had taken from the whale to try and find out why he was so still.

"Morning doctor can we meet for lunch I have something very important to tell you?

No I cannot tell you over the phone what I have to say will change your whole life being dramatic you think? well let's see. I'll pick you up at 1pm!"

Then a thought came to him as he now owned this Oceanarium he was going to have it painted today, the whole place. He made some calls, offered top rates he wanted everything painted ruby red the colour of Tibetan monk's robes and it was to be a nonstop job 24 hours a day till it was done.

Then he called a friend in Dharmsala and ordered 35 large tangkhas of all the major deities Guru Rinpoche, Padmasambhava, Avalokitesvara, Tara white and green, and all the other ones as well yab yum, Vajradhara. Then 13 tangkas of each of the previous Dharma Lamas Then he ordered a huge statue of Tara from the same shop and then 108 smaller Shakyamuni buddhas,2 huge Tibetan trumpets, cymbals, drums, trumpets and incense holders and all the paraphernalia he could think of to equip a fully functional temple. He arranged for them to be delivered to his plane without delay. He may be wrong but he had a feeling that the Oceanarium was soon to become a global focus point for Tibetan Buddhism and so he was going to transform it into a temple which would surround the pool where the Whale would be.

Jonny picked up Geraldine as arranged and drove her a short distance away from the Oceanarium to a shaded area where there was a great view of the ocean and unpacked a picnic with a variety of salad things, cheeses breads and a bottle of white wine.

"This is nice, I love picnics they are my favourite!" she exclaimed excitedly.

"I wanted to speak to you in the open vastness of the sky away from other people."

"Why that sounds deep and meaningful what is this great life changing secret?" she said half mockingly. "Well there is no way around it so I will dive straight in and fill in the details after..." and so he told her who the Whale was to be and what function it would serve and how he had arrived at the astonishing conclusion and that tomorrow the High Lamas with the State Oracle would arrive and in the meantime there was much to do."You gotta be kidding me, no way absolutely no effing way is that possible, the Whale is not the 15th Dharma Lama that is next level hocus pocus." Geraldine said incredulously taking a big swig of her wine. She stared out across the ocean for a moment "no way, it's not even possible?" she snorted.

"Well it is actually through a mystical process known as transmigration, His Holiness even used to say that because the Chinese were trying to destroy Tibetan Buddhism because they were threatened by it he may not come back at all or come back as an insect or an animal, I was there when he said that everyone thought he was joking. But apart from that look at these photos two monks went to Tibet in my jet to a place the State Oracle had directed them and this is what they found." Geraldine looked at the photos and skimmed the report on the Terma. She was a scientist and she needed evidence, credible evidence. This was very, very strange and was stretching her ability to process.

"O my God ..!" was all she could say.

"Geraldine my feeling is that you are not here by mistake and I want you to look after the whale whose name according to the ancient script we found is Kundun. Will you do that, I have rented you a bungalow nearby, a car and anything you need you can have.?

The health of Kundun is of paramount importance. How is he by the way what did your test come up with?"

"He is fine, blood fine, vital signs all fine he is just being still but he must eat today or I will be worried.'

"What does he eat?" Jonny had not thought of this. "Kundin will eat between 140 to 240 pounds of food perday, primarily herring, capelin, salmon and mackerel, preferably fresh though frozen is OK." She replied.

"Geraldine please will you accept this job?"

"Yes..I will but I am here for Kundun and I have to tell you that I don't share or have any knowledge of the belief's that you talk of so count me out of the circus".It felt clear to her yes she was here to look after Kundun that she could handle.

They sat in silence gazing out at the ocean for a while lost in thought when Jonny said" what the, what is that over there are they whales I don't believe it?"

"Yes it's quite common this time of year whales and dolphins pass by here on their way to Antartica." nevertheless there was a wonderfully auspicious feeling seeing them in the wild and so close. Geraldine looked at Jonny who caught her gaze and held it smiling for a while before she looked down a little flushed.

Chapter 6

Dorje Lama, Sonam Tulku, Rinpoche some High Lamas and the State Oracle Choden Guten set off to the airport to fly in Jonny Tibet's Gulfstream2 to Byron Bay on the eastern coast of Australia.

Choden Gluten who had never flown before was still asleep when they arrived to pick her up but it didn't take long for her to get ready and they all set off.

During the long flight there was much silence as the monks prayed and chanted internally for the success of their extraordinary mission. That was until Choden Guten woke up with a raging headache and a great thirst. She found a drinks cabinet in which was some fine liquor the like of which she had never tasted. Everyone knew what was going to happen, there was no avoiding it any minute now Choden was going to get leary. But a strange thing happened after her third glass of vintage brandy she started to shake uncontrollably her eyes rolling up into her head as she went into trance. The monks gathered around her trying to contain her gesticulations, then a voice came through her quite unlike her own, it sounded uncannily like the 14th Dharma Lama "listen carefully I am in Kundun, he is my next incarnation, I will pick the objects of my previous life through Choden, then make quick preparations for my enthronement. Be careful as usual there are those who will not want the Dharma to flourish." with that Choden Guten convulsed and collapsed into a deep sleep for the rest of the flight!

On arrival there was a fracas at the customs and immigration Choden Guten got impatient waiting to be cleared and started to abuse the official a big man with hard eyes,

"That man is as dumb as a bag of hammers!" she called out at which point he came forward approached Choden Guten and whispered into her ear. Whatever he said caused her to burst out into hysterical laughter," I love this place, these people are so civilised!" "Choden what did he say to you?'asked Sonam Tulku she whispered "he said I hope your ears turn into arseholes and shit all over your shoulders!"

The Tulku didn't get it at that point the official let everyone through smiles all round and a wave for

Chuden Guten.

After a short drive they arrived at the Oceanarium which was being transformed into a temple complex being painted burgundy. Mobile homes had been rented for the monks and the kitchens were functioning. Jonny Tibet saw them approaching so got everyone out to welcome them with white scarfs that Tibetans give each other as a sign of respect.

Then he led them to see Kundun they walked quietly in single file and stood before the underground window that allowed viewers to see the whale who was now swimming around and eating after his still fast.

As they stood there in awe of this extraordinary mammal Kundun came and with a deft flick of his tale soaked them all with a great splash. Everyone was laughing and there was a very happy feeling that was touching everyone.

Dorje Lama told Jonny Tibet what the State Oracle had said whilst channeling the 14th Dharma Lama on the plane and so it was agreed that tomorrow morning ther would be an inauguration of the Temple space and the Buddhas, following which the test to see if Kundun the whale could pick out the objects from his previous incarnation.

The preparations were intense with great activity all the artefacts which they had brought with them. The great golden Tara, the 108 Buddhas, the hanging tangkas were all positioned and the complex began to take shape as dawn broke.

Kundun was fed a large breakfast by Geraldine and then proceeded to swim around and around the large tank as if spinning a great prayer wheel.

At nine all the workers and lay people had taken their seats and then from afar came the sound of high pitched Tibetan trumpets announcing the approach of the High lamas and monks wearing their tall yellow hats, carrying a great ornamental umbrella. A symbol of great auspiciousness. As they came into the underground viewing area Kundun swum up to the window and became still, the atmosphere was electric and being filmed by one of Jonny old friends from his movie making days.

The procession stopped in front of Kundun then all the monks took their places on mats in rows and a litany of prayers and chants started. Every now and then bells were rung and the great deep trumpets were blown clearing the space and inviting all the Buddhas to come and be present.

Then two monks brought in a table with four bowls, four pairs of glasses, four malas and four pens. Next to each one was a number. Then Chunden Guten the state oracle was brought in wearing a blind fold and sat down facing Kundun with her back to the table.

Jonny whispered to Geraldine that now the Oracle, who she had met earlier and actually felt rather drawn to, would pick out the objects of the previous Dharma Lama, receiving direction from Kundun.

It was a tense moment everything depended on this working, there was a silence nothing happened, more silence still nothing happened Chonden was muttering something, then suddenly Kundun released a jet of air and Choden Guten sat up and gave a mighty shiver and shouted OM AH HUNG VAJRA GURU PADMA SIDDHI HUNG! Then tapping her silver breast plate she said: "Glasses 4, mala 2, bowls 1 and none of the pens belong to the Dharma Lama!".

Dorje Lama looked at his list and consulted with another high Lama they looked at each other smiling, radiant, overjoyed because Kundun had indeed chosen all the objects that were his in his previous incarnation as the Dharma Lama.

He turned to the assembled people and solemnly announced" Kundun the whale through the state oracle has chosen the objects correctly and so in three days time on the new moon 49 days after his passing from the body of the 14th Dharma Lama we will perform the requisite prayers and pujas to install Kundun as the 15th Dharma Lama as prophesied in the recently discovered ancient texts. To this end we will send out invitations to the Dalai Lama and the heads of all lineages and other relevant dignitaries to come here for that auspicious event." There was clapping and cheering and Kundun seemed to be smiling as well!

As Sonam Tulku left the underground temple he could not help but notice Rinpoche on the phone in the shadows at the back of the room. He had a sinking feeling.

Chapter 7

On the morning on of the enthronement the first to arrive were four coach loads of Tibetans who lived in Brisbane. They had made the long drive overnight and immediately set about decorating the temple with flowers and garlands and elaborate butter lamps. They brought boxes of sweets, fruit of all kinds and rows and rows of butter lamps being set out in fine order.

Prayer flags had been hung from the highest point in the public gallery and fluttered auspiciously in the light breeze.

By eleven all the guests had taken their places in the underground temple, one wall of which was the glass window that allowed a view of the great tank that Kundun lived in. The rest of the guests were seated in the above ground viewing area.

The press release had caused quite a stir and

there were a couple of news crews with their trucks and cameras who had turned up to record this very unusual event. However the Chinese had also released a press release decrying the enthronement as the pathetic display of a dying culture riddled with superstition. They categorically said that under no circumstances would they acknowledge a whale as the new Dharma Lama and to do so would make them look as ridiculous as the Tibetans now did.

The ceremony was just about to begin when there was a stirring in the audience and a strange sound people looked around and there at the entrance were twenty three Aboriginal indigenous tribes people wearing shorts and not much else they had smeared white ash on their faces and wore red headbands. They were an impressive sight with older men leading the women and youngsters.

"G'day we are here because we're invited in the dreaming by the great whale to witness his big day, we have known for hundreds of years that one day when the sun of good sense is not shining the whale and man would merge their mind together. Today is that day." They were shown to the front where they sat on the floor in front of the tank window.

Then the ceremony started with a procession of

monk's wearing their traditional yellow hats blowing trumpets and carrying the ceremonial umbrellas followed by the High Lamas.

At one point the great fifteen foot trumpets which had a very deep resonance were being blown and the Aboriginals joined in blowing their didgeridoos which made an impressive sound, clearing the space and inviting all into the presence.

During the ceremony which lasted several hours every so often monks would come rushing in with tea and snacks for everyone.

After the main invocation Kundun came up to the window and seemed to be smiling it was at this time that the high Lamas, the monks and the ley people all filed past the newly enthroned 15th Dharma Lama offering gifts, of small buddhas, auspicious gold objects, money and scarves. Bowing in front of the whale as they made their offering. It certainly seemed to be that he was acknowledging each one as they passed. At the end the Aboriginals who had not brought any offerings came up together and put their faces and hands on the window and Kundun moved right up to the glass and connected with them.

There was a great feeling in the room and there were tears in the eyes of some, tears of great joy that something so wonderful and beyond the normal scope of the mind could be happening.

Everyone returned to their seats and there was a moment of silence followed by the unmistakeable sound of thunder right over head out of nowhere, unseasonable clouds had formed and it was raining.

There was a flash of lightening and suddenly all the lights went out and the underground Temple became darkened. The audience stirred but calmed as it became clear that Kundun, who was now enthroned as the 15th Dharma Lama seemed to be glowing, it was literally his whole body was emitting an aura of light. Just as it became visible the lights came back on and every one cheered.

There was a meal offered upstairs and as everyone filed from the temple and came into the open air the rain had passed and a beautiful rainbow girdled the complex.

Geraldine who had been in the ceremony, watching from the back, really did not know what to make of it all. She had conflicting feelings and her scientific mind was reacting to all the strange customs and superstitions. One of her migraine headaches was developing, she knew the signs, she was yawning a lot, the sounds and colours were getting too loud and bright, she seemed to feel euphoric one minute an depressed the next, so she decided to leave the celebrations and retire to her bungalow and rest in a darkened room and hope that the coming storm in her brain would not be too severe. As she walked away from the complex she heard a TV commentator saying. "so there it is we have a new Dharma Lama enthroned today in the body of a whale,in what may have been one of the most extraordinary things to ever have happened in Australia."

"You're not kidding" she thought as she headed for home.

She collapsed on her bed and reached for her medication there was only one left, she needed three minimum.That was it, she burst into tears and lay there sobbing until eventually she drifted off into the comforting arms of sleep.

She found herself dreaming in front of Kundun who was talking to her saying " give me your headache come now and swim with me, come now and swim with me!". With a start she awoke with a full recollection of the dream and a pounding headache which seemed to reach down deep into her brain. She had no room in her mind to resist so she got up and made her way to the tank where Kundun was. As she arrived he surfaced and blew a jet of air, he looked at her as if to say 'come on then'. Taking off her t-shirt and jeans, in her underwear.she dived into the water. It felt wonderful to be weightless and free. A thought occurred to her that her headache had completely gone. Kundun came towards her and stopped. She felt a surge of love, Kundun was definitely smiling at her. She saw a light coming from the underground temple, butter lamps flickering, she dived down and saw Jonny sitting in meditation. Another wave of love arose within her and she realised that right from the start she had been resisting the love she naturally felt for him. She felt she had known him forever and her fear had made her closed and distant when in fact she wanted nothing more than to be in his arms. At this point Kundun came from beneath her and gave her a friendly nudge that sent her up to the surface. She knew that he was telling her to go and see Jonny right now.

She got out and put her clothes on without drying and ran down the stairs into the temple, Jonny heard her coming and got up they met in front of the tank window. Geraldine ran towards him and gave him a long embrace. They were silent for a while then she pulled back and told him "I have to tell you that I love you and that I have been distant because I am frightened of being hurt."

Jonny looked at her and truly smiled "well thats

great because you know what? I loved you from the moment I first saw you!" They kissed for an immeasurable moment and when they opened their eyes Kundun was there watching them.

Geraldine told Jonny all that had happened as they walked back to her bungalow where they spent the night together, experiencing, as so many humans have done before them, the miracle of love's dawning.

Geraldine felt amazing something happened to her when she dived in the tank with Kundun it was as if all her burdens had fallen away and that now she was free to be who she really was. Her migraine had completely gone and she felt so vital and free. She spoke to Jonny telling of how different she felt after being in the water with Kundun. She maybe could understand it if she has a big believer but she was not yet something definitely had happened to her.

Chapter 8

Sonam Tulku was worried he knew that Rinpoche had been avoiding him and he knew why. So he went and sought him out.

"Rinpoche why are you avoiding me?"

"I am very busy setting things up why would I avoid you?" he replied

"Rinpoche tell me, have you contacted the Chinese man again? Who were you calling after the Test?'

"No one, well just a friend!"

"Rinpoche give me your phone if you have nothing to hide show me your recent calls!"

At this point Rinpoche knew the game was up for him not to show his recent calls would be as good as saying he was guilty.

"O Tulku I admit I was calling the Chinese spy again he told me to tell him the result of the test, he sent me a photo, my niece was in an accident and has broken her leg. He was showing me what happens when I don't cooperate.I didn't know what to do I feel so terrible for what I have done." He stared at the floor full of shame. "Look Rinpoche I understand I can see what terrible position you were in next time don't hide it from me tell me and maybe we can use it to our advantage!

Come with me now we must make a press release telling of the prophecy of what the 15th Dharma Lama is to accomplish."

So they sat and surveyed the notes taken and the translation made by the Office of Antiquities in Dharmsala.

The prophecy of the life of the 15th Dharma Lama will be composed of five Miraculous events:

1. The manner of his reincarnation in the whale Kundun.

2. The healing of body, speech and mind.

3. The teaching

4. His association with other whales

5. The manner of his departure.

" The first one has happened but what is the meaning of the second how can a whale heal anyone?" asked Rinpoche at that moment Jonny and Geraldine walked in overhearing what

Rinpoche asked. Jonny said "we have a feeling that His Holiness is charging the water so that it creates powerful healings, Geraldine swam with Kundun yesterday and immediately a vicious migraine headache completely disappeared."

"That's amazing, we should find some people with different ailments to see if it was by chance or if it actually works on everybody" said Sonar Tulku.

So they enquired of the Tibetan visitors who still had not left the complex if there was anyone who needed healing of anything. A woman came forward with a skin disease which made her skin peel and itch. Another person came forward with a terrible back pain that would not allow them to stand straight and upright. A young girl who was suffering deep depression and would not eat anything or talk to anyone was lead forward by her mother.

So Sonam Tulku explained what was happening and what the theory was and then lead then to the topside of the tank and told them to prepare to enter the tank. First up was the woman with the skin disease she entered the water gently and submerged herself and was a bit alarmed when Kundun turned toward her, she swam back to the steps

"O my god! o my god! My arms are completely

clear, the red blotches and peeling skin! Look! look it has completely cleared!" she exclaimed immediately prostrating on the ground before Kundun.

Then the man whose back was in terrible pain entered the water with difficulty and determination, inspired by what had just happened to the lady. He lowered himself in and immediately felt relief as he floated in the tank.

He figured though that it was probably just the effect of gravity so he swam back to the steps and said "I feel some relief but I think it's just gravity "then he realised he was walking up the step with a straight back and now out of the water he stood straight with no pain for the first time in six years. He was overjoyed and started to dance with joy at the miraculous occurrence." Long live the Dharma Lama! Long Live the Dharma Lama!"

At that point the mother of the young girl pushed her forward but she did not want to go in so Geraldine stepped forward "come with me and let's go in together Kundun is full of love and will not hurt anyone, come on!"

So they entered the tank and then they both fully immersed themselves when they surfaced the young girl looked at Geraldine and started to laugh "I understand now my misery was bound to end because everything changes and it just did! "She exclaimed full of joy "gosh I am so very hungry!"' everyone laughed with joy and Kundun released a great jet of air and swum in a circle as if taking a lap honour.

"This is amazing" said Jonny "we must be sure to film and document every single miracle that happens otherwise we will never be believed"

"Yes that's a great idea I will arrange that if you would like.' said Geraldine enthusiastically.

"We need to let people know that their suffering can end and to come and be healed!"

Over the next days news of the miracles spread like wildfire through the Tibet community in Australia and people started arriving with all kinds of conditions to swim with Kundun and be healed.

One of the first to arrive was a woman who had been diagnosed with pancreatic cancer and was due to die within few months. She came and plunged in to the water and immediately after was seen by a doctor who could find no trace of the cancer.

People decided to stay and help out organising the Healings and building accommodation cooking and doing other jobs so that the complex could manage the crowds that would inevitably arrive.

The monks started continuous chanting in the Temple for the welfare of all beings and many of those who had been healed went down to the Temple after wards and said they experienced profound meditation states as well as being healed. it appeared to be that the healing was total clearing the diseases from the body and the mind allowing the enlightened state to shine through.

Then there came a busload of people in wheelchairs who had dysfunctional limbs, it seemed impossible to think that they could be healed but no one was to be turned away so a winch was built over the edge of the pool and one by one they were lowered into the water and as they came out they were introduced to walking and like new born ponies pretty soon they were finding their way and gaining their balance and doing the impossible, they were walking.

Then quite soon a heroin addict in a very bad way stumbled into the complex asking for help, he was lead up to the queue and then when his turn came he plunged into the water it was as if he fizzed but a darkness left him and he came out looking radiantly healthy. He was crying because he knew what had happened to him. He was shown to the Temple where he committed his life to the Buddha, the Dharma and the Sangha. He sat to meditate and immediately achieved a deep state of profound peace and knew that now for him all was forever well, he had been saved and so would become a monk and take the sacred vows.

The extraordinary goings on at the Oceanarium which was now named the Temple of Miracles reached the TV news and then the number of people coming rose dramatically. A security firm had to be hired to manage the crowds and keep order. Vendors set up and with all the help offered by the healed, everyone's needs were met, donations were pouring in and there was a rapid expansion.

People with mental disorders schizophrenics, psychotics the unbalanced were all dramatically healed and established in deep peace.

Then one day there was bus that arrived from Brisbane carrying thirty blind people who had flown in from Korea. They were shown to the queue and one by one, as their turn came, they plunged into the highly charged water with Kundun and all of them had their sight restored some had been blind since birth. It was all so unbelievable and wonderful the blind being healed and given sight, the deaf hearing and the lame dancing what great joy filled that place. The world had never seen anything like it.

In Beijing members of the Ministry of State Security were meeting to decide how to deal with this unprecedented turn of events which was beginning to undermine all their efforts of disempowering indigenous Tibetans by destroying their culture and religion. These so called miracles must be stopped immediately was the general agreement and intention of the meeting.

"That whale must be dealt with in a terminal way" shouted the commissar Chang Ping.

"I don't care what it takes I want it dead, no whale, no problem so kill it!." he raged.

Ramjem the Chinese spy who was trying to handle Rinpoche, received a text from his boss commanding him to take out the whale using any means necessary as a matter of extreme urgency. After thinking about it for some time it occurred to him that the best way to do this was by hacking into the water control system that regulated the flow of new water into the tank and in the middle of the night to simply empty the tank and by dawn when people awoke the whale would be dead, a terrible accident.

As part of his basic training he had been shown

how to hack into any basic system and it was a puzzle that he loved to solve, he liked to think there was no system he could not hack. It did not take him long to get into the system and isolate the program for the tank water regulation. There was a timer so he reprogrammed it to go into full flush mode at 1:30 am which would take half an hour and allow several hours of emptiness before likely detection. He felt pleased with himself and figured that this action against the whale would probably bring some considerable benefit to his career.

When he had done this he went out and ran into Rinpoche who was distraught and deeply conflicted " I can not help you any more, I just can't, you have seen that something very special is happening here and people are having life transforming experiences and you must know that the whale is something very special. I can't help you anymore!"

"I know nothing except that some superstitious Tibetans have got the media believing in their stupid nonsense and we are witnessing the placebo effect and no miracle. It's simply ridiculous nonsense! Anyway don't worry, I don't need your help anymore my work here is nearly done".retorted Ramjem.

That night there was no moon and after an

exhausting day where hundreds of people had become healed The Temple of Miracles was quiet. Butter lamps flickered in the underground Temple and the golden image of Arya Tara glowed in golden light.

In the security office at the gates of the complex the guard had snoozed off and would not be relieved until 6 am. All was quiet.

At 1:30am the automatic water flush activated and this was witnessed by Ramjem who was monitoring it from his computer in his car nearby. Suddenly a red light started flashing on the screen. "OPEN FLUSH PORTAL MANUALLY". He immediate knew what this meant, the old system was dysfunctional and he would have to open the flush gate manually, he had seen a cranking system when he was scouting out the area a few days ago. So he ran over to the complex, ducked under the security office window and went upstairs into the public viewing area at the back of which was the cranking system to open the flush gate and empty the water into the ocean. He applied his strength but it was not budging, then he saw there was a safety catch he flicked it open and then cranked up the flush gate, the water started to empty from the tank and pour into the ocean.

He went over to the tank to check the water

levels which were sinking fast as he predicted, when suddenly Kundun's head appeared looking at him directly.

Ramjem felt startled as if he had been caught but he had a job to do and he would do it.

He waited in the shadows for a while then heard someone coming, he ducked and then ran for it, the pool was nearly empty. As he passed by the tank Kundun emerged again which distracted Ramjem, he tripped and fell, banging his head against a supporting pillar. He was knocked clean out and lay there blood trickling from a nasty cut on his head.

Choden Guten woke up with a start completely awake she knew something was very wrong and that the 15th Dharma Lama was in great danger. She had had this feeling before all those years ago the night that the Chinese soldiers had come to arrest the 14th Dharma Lama. She climbed out of bed and rushed to the tank which was by now virtually empty of water. She saw a light in the security office and ran over, when she saw the security officer dosing she gave him a great kick "wake up you good for nothing, sound the alarm there is no water in the tank!".

Minutes later Jonny and Geraldine had arrived and some monks had also woken up, Jonny went to the tank controls and turned the water on it.

"How long is it going to take to fill up? Kundun is already having respiratory problems, he must have been here out of the water for quite while!"

"Maybe an hour or two till he is covered and more to fill up completely!" replied Jonny.S

It was then that Gerladine saw the Chinese spy Ramjem lying unconscious in the shadows, she rushed over and saw he was still alive.

"Jonny look at this man do you know him? he is unconscious" she said.

He came over and searched the Chinese man's pockets, a Chinese passport and a mobile phone. Jonny picked up the man's right hand index finger and placed it on the access button the phone lit up. He was in, Jonny checked the phone log:

"This is Ramjem Chung and he is almost certainly a spy judging by the calls he has been making to Beijing and by the looks of things he was on a mission to kill Kundun".

"We have to help him let's put him in the tank with Kundun?" suggested Geraldine.

So some monks lifted him up over the edge into the few feet of water that Kundun was now beginning to float in. They rolled him over without ceremony and immediately he came back to consciousness, the wound on his head had largely disappeared. He looked up into the eyes of the monks who were holding him and saw Kundun behind them. He knew something had happened to him something wonderful, he could feel the love emanating from the monks. He was so glad to be alive. As he stood up in the water his heart was overwhelmed with good feelings that he had never felt before.

"I have made such a great mistake, my whole life has been a huge mistake and to think that I was intent on killing this amazing being, oh dear please help me find the true way." A senior monk took his hand and they left the tank area. Later Ramjem Chung, the former Chinese spy, took vows and became a Buddhist monk and two days later realised the true nature of reality,his mind and Karma having been purified by his association with the 15th Dharma Lama.

The tank was filled and Geraldine checked to see that all was well with Kundun after his attempted assassination. From this experience things changed and there was to be tighter security and the identities of all who came had to be checked. The thought of loosing Kundun made everyone realise how much they had come to love him.

Chapter 9

After some days Choden Guten had a dream she was a young girl wearing white coming from the sea approaching a great temple with a great sense of purpose, She knew what it meant, she had to take a plunge with Kundun and then channel his teaching.

So early one morning she went before the Temple opened and taking off her white bathrobe she entered the pool. Kundun came over and she knew to hold his fin. He swam her around and as he did she began to laugh and laugh having more fun than she had ever had in her whole life.

Kundun dropped her off by the steps and there she floated on her back and as she relaxed she experienced that her mind was one with Kundun. As she climbed out of the tank she felt a great calmness and a certainty that all was well and the what would be would be.

On her way back to her room she saw Dorje Lama who was taken aback by her appearance." Choden Guten you look so young and radiant how do you feel this fine morning?' "I feel wonderful and ready to channel the teachings of the 15th Dharma Lama." "The monks are beginning the preliminary prayers and the teaching is scheduled for 11 am" Dorje Lama replied happy to find the State Oracle looking so well.

Everyone started to assemble the High Lamas, the monks the ley people and the film crews. There was much chanting and cymbals crashing, trumpets blowing as an atmosphere of auspiciousness was created in the traditional Tibetan Buddhist way.

Then Choden Guten was processed into the Temple with a High Lama at each side she was wearing a splendid colourful and highly embroidered ornamental dress with her silver disc over her heart. There was a small throne prepared for her infront of the big window behind which was Kundun.

As she sat down the deep trumpets stopped and there was a profound silence filled with presence. The 15th Dharma Lama slowly swam up behind Choden and became still.

The High Lama came over with an ornamental crown off feathers and jewels, the Crown of the State Oracle it was placed on Chodren Gutens head and she immediately shuddered her eyes rolled up into her head and she entered a deep state of trance. The other high Lama placed the microphone near her mouth. The anticipation in the full temple was palpable, moments past.

"All beings exist in the same moment and the idea that we are separate independent beings having a substantial separate self is a very persistent illusion. Deep penetrative insight will show us that no such self exists. Most beings have minds that are, how shall we say, locked which means that they only hear their own thoughts and only experience their own state of consciousness. Through practice of meditation and the guidance of an authentic teacher one may come to unlock the mind and this has several stages.

In the first stage of unlocking the mind one becomes aware in deep stillness that I am not the thinker. It is clearly seen that thoughts arise of their own accord. How shall we say? They think themselves, What determines what kind of thoughts we will think in any moment is given by who we are being in that moment. For example if we are being angry spontaneously arising angry thoughts will come as long as that quality of being persists and so forth. In the first stage of Unlocking the Mind we become freed from the mental realm and the bondage of identifying as the thinker. Until this unlocking has happened wisdom is only conceptual. Wisdom is the term given to ideas and concepts that have a quality of clarity, insight and understanding.

On the second stage of Unlocking the Mind it is seen that there are no walls between the consciousness of one being and that of another. Resting as this unlocked pure mind one can feel the consciousness and mental activity of another. It is from this view that the saying 'the mind of the master and the student are one' is experienced as true. When this is realised experientially then the Master can transmit without obstruction the teachings on a vibrational and transcendental way without words or concepts directly from mind to mind.

Here it is also seen that all creatures have a unique frequency upon which they resonate and through which the knowledge of their kind is transmitted generation to generation. One realises that one is part of a living organism that is all life, every part of which is communicating to every other in an interdependent dance of life. It is because humanity has lost this experience of being one with all life that it feels disconnected from it and so takes no care of it. I am part of the Nature I observe. In the second stage there is access to the expanded memory of the Collective consciousness.

The Dharma Lama can and does choose how he will reincarnate because he has developed these stages of Unlocking of the Mind. He can project his mind stream wherever he wants and on this occasion his attention was drawn to a Whale by a set of causes and conditions to complex to unravel.

Once the unlocking has happened and the mental realm transcended altogether then Wisdom takes its true form as a field of pure knowingness without a subject who knows or an object of knowledge.

The phenomenal world is seen as non different having no substantial existence.

So how shall we say? It's not real.

What conditions must be present for us to say something is real because things certainly seem real to us. For something to be real it must be born of something real. A real thing cannot emerge from what is unreal The car you dream of when asleep will not be parked outside in the morning when you wake! What is unreal. Also can have no constituent parts it must be one complete independent thing. Also something that is real must have an edge which nothing does as what appears as an edge to something actually is a blurred mass of subatomic particles. Another determining factor of what is real is that it must not evolve or change from one thing to another. So if we look at these factors we might ask what is it that has these attributes? Is there anything?

So to be clear states of consciousness, mental states and formations, moods, feelings and emotions, all things, phenomena, objects and the dramas of life are not real because they do not have the requisite factors.

The third and final stage of the Unlocking the Mind is when we unlock the mind from the clinging to all of the above and without holding onto anything at all recognise ourselves as unborn, undying and unchanging awareness, unassociated with what changes and having no constituent parts.

This is suchness, this is pure presence, this is unchanging reality and it is the substratum of all life. Everywhere equally present, not evolving, inconceivable and ungraspable.

Consider these words carefully and you will become free from mental hindrances and delusions becoming again the enlightened truth.

May all beings hearing this extraordinary teaching not be dismayed but liberated by it.!

May all beings realise conscious universal enlightenment.!

May all beings be happy and joyful!

Let us sit in the Silence of Buddha Mind and Unlock the mind for some moments."

As the assembled crowd sat an extraordinary peace and presence came over them, all thinking slowed down and stopped, complete stillness and in that great silence the luminosity became increasingly manifest both within and without.Gradually everyone's mind was fully pacified and the essence, the very ground of being, the unchanging awareness became all that was.

Kundun the !5th Dharma Lama was floating motionless in the tank as time seemed to stop and the timelessness of the unchanging pervaded the atmosphere of that sanctified place.

Many beings gained their liberation in that great assembly never going back into the erroneous idea that they were the thinker and remaining simply as awareness itself.

Everyone seemed to open their eyes together as Kundun turned and swam off to another part of the tank. The Oracle calmly opened her eyes. It was over, quietly people left but there were many who remained in deep and profound rapture of inner cognition for the rest of the day.

Chapter 10

The complex was dealing with very large numbers of people and the extraordinary healings continued unabated. A large marquee structure was created where people could sit and meditate after their healing because it was noticed that it was both the body and the mind that was healed. People who had very agitated and disturbed minds found that they were able to enter deep absorption states usually only felt by adepts.

So many people were desperate to be healed there was increasing pushing and shoving and no amount of security seemed to be able to keep the hordes of arriving visitors in check.

Geraldine had been watching Kundun's well being carefully and she had come to a conclusion which she had decided to share with Jonny when they met for lunch.

"There is something I have to say that you are

not going to like Jonny!"

"Sounds ominous, go on then!"

"Well I am worried about Kundun, I am not sure he can take much more of this constant demand on his energies." she said.

"What makes you think that?"

"Well Orca whales have as you know a fin on their back and normally that fin is firm and erect bit I have noticed in the past weeks that Kundun fin has become floppy which to my thinking is a sign of being run down. Also I have noticed that he is developing some kind of boil on his under side, it's hard to tell but it looks as if poison is gathering. This is another sign of being run down, he is a creature that needs to swim unrestricted in the ocean". she paused,

"Jonny it is my feeling that we should release Kundun back into the ocean from where he came before he develops chronic and incurable symptoms."

"You are joking we have the most amazing thing ever and you want to let it go?" exclaimed Jonny.

"Jonny it's not a thing it's a living being, Kundun the 15th Dharma Lama and." suddenly she was interrupted by Choden Gutens "She is right I had a dream last night Kundun came he said he has one more miracle to perform and he cannot do it here, we must set him free."

The three of them went to see Lama Dorje and although he was not happy he somehow knew this was what must be.

"We will make arrangements for a final puja,Gather all the monks but I think it best if we close the temple temporarily for healing and the public."

Jonny suggested that the best way to release Kundun was to get a crane on the pretext of fixing the roof and lift him out of the tank and place him in the water when the tide was next high.

As it turned out there was no final puja or need for a crane. The following night there was a huge storm, the tail end of a typhoon and the tide was also high. The waves mounted ever higher crashing into the tank, the risen tide lapped at the wall of the tank and as the storm increased it's intensity the waves came crashing into the tank hit the back wall and surged out again and so it was that Kundun waited for the right moment and after a great wave hit the back wall of the tank he swam with it and was literally carried over the tank wall into the shallows of the raging ocean and gone as he had come.

Epilogue

It was of course a huge shock and a thing of great sadness for everyone when it was discovered that Kundun the 15th Dharma Lama had disappeared in the storm. No-one quite knew what to do, should they look for him, accept the fact or what?

After a while thing's calmed down and the extra ordinary occurrence of a Dharma Lama incarnating in a whale slipped into history. The monks returned to Dharmsala. Jonny and Geraldine remained in the bungalow for some time then one moonlit night Jonny asked Geraldine to marry him and she happily consented.

They went off to live in New York though Jonny did not have the heart to sell the Oceanarium.

A couple of years passed and Jonny and Geraldine were again in Australia for one thing and another and so decided to visit the Temple as part of their trip. Geraldine had some friends who were marine biologists in the area so she called them. What they told her she found very surprising they said that yesterday 100 whales had passed by Byron Point but had not been seen passing the next point which means they must be in the area still. It occurred to her that a hundred whales was a large number to be moving together on their way down to the Antarctic. She told Jonny so they decided to charter a boat and some underwater gear and go have a look to see what was happening.

It was a beautiful day as they set off to where the whales had last been seen and spent some time cruising around looking for any spumes or any sign at all of the whales presence.

There was nothing so Jonny suggested that they just stop where they were and get the diving gear on and just dive in. They swam down not really expecting much after a while Geraldine started signalling to Jonny to place which they both started swimming to a ridge. To their surprise there was a whale resting on the ocean floor as they came around an outcrop of coral they saw the most astonishing sight a hundred whales all facing the whale on the ridge and all apparently not breathing resting on the ocean floor. Geraldine signalled to Jonny to go up to the surface.

They were both very excited when they surfaced, "That was Kundun, that was definitely Kundun!" exclaimed Geraldine excitedly.

"Yes it was but what about the other whales all facing him and still. I think Kundun has taught the whales to meditate! I am not kidding I think that is what they were doing!" said Jonny.

"I have never seen anything like that before that's amazing, they appear not to be breathing."

"Well when humans meditate and become still their breathing also slows right down almost to a complete standstill".

"I think we should leave them to it and wait in the boat for them to finish maybe we will see Kudun" Jonny agreed any way they were running out of air.

They got back in the boat and relaxed in the heat of the afternoon. Suddenly Jonny who had been scanning the horizon with the binoculars 'well goodness me look who has turned up on the beach!" he said handing Geraldine the binoculars. "Oh my god it's the Aboriginals that came to the inauguration, they seem to be sitting in a semi circle with their didgeridoos, I wonder what has brought them here again after all this time, it a long way from their tribal grounds" she said.

"Well one thing you can be sure with those guys is that they are always where they are supposed to be when they are supposed to be there." said Jonny. "something is happening".

At that exact moment a whale surfaced with a

great snort and spume, then another rising high into the air and crashing down and then another and another all rising up with a great force and crashing down again with a huge splash. All of them were surfacing at the same time, soaring into the air and crashing down again. They started to create a circle made of surging splashing waves then the circle started to rotate in the same direction a massive dance from these majestic creatures had Jonny and Geraldine completely amazed. The collective energy of all these whales seemed to be gathering and their momentum was increasing all of sudden a whale ascended from the depths with tremendous force right in the middle of the circle, it soared clean out of the water up into the sky there was a brilliant flash of light and an explosion of colours, rainbows in all directions and then nothing, it completely disappeared.

The whales returned to the depths and swam off soon nothing remained.

"What the hell was that that just happened? Did you see what Kundun did?"

"Yes I may be wrong but I think we just witnessed his last miracle his disappearance into a rainbow body."said Jonny awestruck.

"Whats that?"

"We Tibetans believe that enlightened beings don't die in the normal way they can just vanish into pure essence, the suchness from where they came. It is said when they do this they just vanish in a flash of rainbow light."

The Aboriginals where dancing wildly on the beach and Jonny and Geraldine knew exactly how they felt.

The 15th incarnation of the Dharma Lama was over.

(After the ideas for this story came I met His Holiness the Dalai Lama at Glastonbury Festival. Afterwards he walked off to visit a Greenpeace exhibition. The last I saw of him he was walking into the mouth of a huge whale, the entrance to the exhibit. I took this as an auspicious sign! Long Live the Dalai Lama!)

Made in the USA
Middletown, DE
31 August 2021